Money
Matters

WRITTEN BY DENISE LEBLANC

Produced by:

FriesenPress

Suite 300 – 990 Fort Street
Victoria, BC, Canada V8V 3K2

www.friesenpress.com

Distributed to the trade by The Ingram Book Company

Table of Contents

Introduction

People kept asking me "How do you do it?" Instead of always repeating myself over and over, I decided to write it down. And there it was, my eight-page guide on how to save "MONEY" and also to get the *things* you want out of life. I passed it along to people who wanted to have a better life. Living without having money worries can make you a healthier person.

See, people knew my longtime boyfriend and I weren't making much money with our jobs, and it seemed like we had a great life, a new home, a Corvette, a truck, an SUV, a jet ski, and a cottage. I know it's hard to believe, but it's all about what you do with your money that makes the difference. My eight-page guide called "What School Doesn't Teach You: Simple Budgeting" is a great tool for anyone wanting, and I mean *wanting* to have a better life. It's OK to say "I want it," but a different thing to do it.

Well, 20 years later and here I want to write about MONEY again, mostly because so many people are having a hard time with it. I have written this book that includes my already-written guidebook, plus chapters on what to do from your

20's to your 70's, some business tips, how to go about starting a business (another frequently asked question I get), and the pros and cons of purchasing a franchise as well as looking at retirement, information about rental incomes, bankruptcy, and multiple units. I want to give you a variety of simple information that you may need in life, because where else are you going to get it?

I don't want to just talk about savings. I want to go into detail for people who think they cannot save any money, or for people who are in bad debt, or people who don't know where to begin a budget. I want to walk you through the changes and make you have a better life.

You know, Money never leaves you; you can lose your boyfriend, your family and your friends but money is always going to be a part of your life. Like it or not, that is the reality of life. Money means food and survival. It's not just about saving money; it's about having money to live and, hopefully, making some extra money to enjoy life. It's about changing your way of thinking. Money can be a big part of a couple's arguments, and it can destroy families because people don't RESPECT money.

So let's go find a new, more enriched life....

What Does Money Mean To You?

The first thing I want to ask you is, "What does money mean to you?"

Answer: _____

At the end of the book, come back to this question and see if your answer is the same!

Answer (after reading this book): _____

Here are some of the answers from other people that I have asked.

Ron, age 55 (self-employed contractor) = nothing

Marc, age 54 (painter) = security

Ella, age 12 = something to spend

Drew, age 14 = to save for the future because it's going to be expensive

Bob, age 49 (propane truck driver) = freedom

Danny, age 45 (book store owner) = source of stress or freedom

Donna, age 57 (office worker) = security

Catherine, age 50 (bank financial Adviser) = security

Johanna, age 28 (office clerk) = necessary

Nikki, age 27 (office clerk) = life is not all about money

Chris, age 31 (realtor) = security, family stability

Freda, age 73 (retired office worker) = I can travel

The world of finance is not the most fun or exciting thing for people to do, but the rewards are the fun and exciting things. Changing your ways of spending can make all your dreams come true.

After looking at my list, I see that "security" is popular, so if this is such a big concern why are we not all planning to have money at retirement? Remember, no one wants to be poor.

It's because we are not told by anyone what, how and when to plan for retirement. We must start at an early age.

Chapter 1

What School Doesn't Teach You...
Simple Budgeting

HERE is a simple way to budget your money. This can be used by anyone, even for the people who think they're already on a budget.

Do you think you can't save any money? Think again; even if you believe it's impossible, my budget will show how.

In today's economy you need to know your income status; where do you stand? Do you know how much money you spend in a month? Do you know if you're spending more than you earn? These are questions you need to answer. Your future and your children's futures depend on it. In the past, our parents may not have guided us on how to plan our future, and we didn't learn it in school. We have to change our ways. I have some easy steps that I've used in the past and I am currently using today. If you really want to follow my budget, I will do the impossible and make you save money. Yes, it demands a little sacrificing, but it may not last long; only you will decide. The more you sacrifice, the greater the reward.

BEFORE you start reading, I'm asking you to clear your mind of negative thoughts. Pretend you were just born.

There are a lot of bad habits to break. You may have to cut down on some little pleasures today to enjoy bigger ones later. You will see the day you reach your goals. You will become a lot happier and less stressed over money.

Do you ever think how people lived years ago? How did they live without video games, exercise machines, and computers? Can you imagine living without fast food and cell phones? It seems impossible. Do you know what we need to live on? Food, water and oxygen! The reason I'm saying this is because I want your mind to adjust to the little sacrifices you're going to make today, so you can appreciate all the nice things you will get in the future.

Living Everyday on Small Pleasures

This is what most people do. We take our pay cheques, hopefully pay our bills, and with the rest of the money, we spend it until there is nothing left because we know we have another pay coming. Then we do the same thing with our next pay. But worse, we use credit cards, don't know how much we are spending, and are probably spending more than we are making. I'm sure ¾ of the people don't know if they are spending more than they are making. We spend on little things because we think that we can't afford the expensive things, so we always feel that because we *work hard* all week, we deserve to treat ourselves. **That's it!** We do work hard all week. So we should deserve to have better and nicer things with a stress-free life. These small pleasures can stop you from becoming rich.

This is what I did: I realized one day that I didn't have any money to pay a January payment of $300.00; per chance, I received a $350.00 Christmas bonus at work. That is when I realized how I needed to do something fast. I saved money my entire life. I saved all my babysitting money, but then I met a boyfriend and we were out a lot with friends. I purchased a sports car and got *"lost in life"*. That's what I call it, lost in living life. So that's when I created my budget and changed my lifestyle and my life. After great success, I am delighted to share it with you.

The Budget

Follow this: Write down your **income** in one column (what you bring home). Then write down your **actual payments** for the month in another column. In the payment column write the things you always pay each month like cable, phone, power, car, and mortgage. Take the ones you pay only yearly or quarterly like house and car insurance, water bill, etc., add them up and divide by 12. Of course, some figures will never be the same, so just use an average of what you would spend. This creates a **GOAL. Example:** Whatever dollar value you put for your phone bill, you now know you shouldn't exceed it per month.

Budget Per Month

Income: _____	Payments:
	Cable, TV, Int: _____
	Phone: _____
	Elec/Power: _____
	Insurance (car/home) _____ (if your Ins. is yearly divide in 12)
	Mortgage/Rent: _____
	Car: _____
	Misc. fixed expense: _____
Total Income: _____ - (minus) Total payments: _____	
	Total Amount: (A) () $_____

Now we total each column. Then *income* minus *payments* equals **total amount,** and we know you should be in the plus (+)! This becomes your "A" amount.

Then we create another column. This (B) column below is to work with the money remaining.

Still per month, we list a monthly budget for groceries. Then we would put some money for savings. There is no way I'm going to let you skip this line. I don't care if it's only $10.00 per week, so you would put in $40.00 per month. Do the savings at the end to try to put as much as possible. Everyone's budget will differ. For the MasterCard and Visa, some may do a monthly payment, and some may pay it all every month (*Good for you!* That's what should be done).

Now for groceries: there are so many deals where you buy one product and get the second one free. Do you realize that the second product, which can vary from $1 to $5, is free; with a coupon, you may only get .50 cents off to $1 off. On the buy one get one free, you get the whole product for free, so watch your weekly flyers to get the best and most food for your money.

Expenses per month: Average it out, and this becomes your budget per month to follow so you can make sure not to overspend. Put this money in marked envelopes to store for only these reasons, such as groceries or gas. Keeping cash on you will make you watch your spending; you can't spend money you don't have.

So with the sum of money from the "A" make a budget in these lines.

B.

Groceries: _____

Credit Card: _____

Credit Card: _____

Gas: _____

Savings:_____ (Get your bank to withdraw this amount into a tax-freesaving account or a Guaranteed Income Certificate. It is very Important for you to PAY YOURSELF too!)

Misc.:_____

Misc.:_____

Misc.:_____

(make this an amount you want to save separately to purchase something special. Ex; big TV, new furniture, trip…etc...

Add your column B.

Total (B): _____ Bring total (A)

_____ (- minus) total (B): _____

(This should still be a +…if not you are spending more
than you make and have to cut back in this section.)

Total: _____   Divide   it   by   4= $

_____(C)

This total, divided by four, (C) is your allowance per week
to spend on coffee, cigarettes, alcohol, lunches, lotto tickets,
etc. because these expenses are your rewards. We put some
money for savings already; you should be good. (But everything counts, and if you have some money left from your
allowance, you can save this too, but that's the saver in me). I
would start my allowance on Sundays and get my cash for the
week. If you don't spend it all in one week, you can either do
one of two things:

1. Save the overage somewhere in a can, suitcase, or envelope in the house.
2. Keep it in your wallet for extra money for the next
   week.

> For you strong saving types, like me, you
> should save the extra or put money down on
> your bills. It's also good to purchase items that
> you wanted that cost a small amount of money.

Your budget will change during the first few months while
you're paying off bills. You may not know or keep track of
what you're charging on your credit cards during each month;
therefore, you should be putting a limit on your spending on

your cards so you don't end up spending more than you make, which is the case for some people. That's why we don't get ahead each year.

Most of you probably have credit card payments in the last section (B) to pay. Well, you don't want to keep increasing those debts and keep paying off credit cards all your life, so you shouldn't be spending more than your budget allows you to. You can't or don't need to do everything in life today; you need to know your limits, when to say no or stop spending.

I hear some people say, "There is more of that product at the store." For example: My boyfriend and I were going in the woods in April, and the roads were muddy. My boyfriend put on a new pair of sneakers, and I was looking at him and saying, "Shouldn't you put on some boots?" He had just bought this pair of sneakers, and even if he wore them instead of his boots in the mud, he would say, "There are more sneakers at the store where I purchase them." But if you have that attitude with everything, then you will be purchasing the same products over and over, and, therefore, spending more money. However if you take care of your things, then you can purchase more different products, like things that you need and not be wasting money on the same thing twice. He did put his boots on and was glad because it was very muddy. His attitude of "there is more at the store" is like he doesn't realize you need to make sure it is in the bank first. In today's world and in people's minds, they don't even realize that there is a cap. You can only spend the money you have, but with credit cards, people have no limitations and don't know how much they have to spend. The money tree in the back yard that everyone thinks is growing doesn't have money; it's full of credit card debt. Until you can swipe your card and it is not declined, you're a happy shopper with only the limit of your card and not the limit of your earnings.

One thing that bothers me more than anything is when people have borrowed money from their parents, family, or friends, but they are still out there spending money on clothes, on restaurants, on drinking or smoking. They're putting themselves deeper into bad consumer debt. WHO do you think your friends, family, and parents are? They could go spend their own money on the same things for themselves. Why would they need to give it to you? If you're the person that is giving the money. Stop you are just their life raft. They will never learn if they know there is always money coming from somewhere. You work hard for your money and maybe have some saved, so why give it to someone who didn't save? Yes, I understand that some people are down and out and need the money for rent or food; that is ok. They may have children and/or are trying to work. It is very hard to get ahead, and it is just getting harder all the time. But don't give to someone that doesn't help themselves and takes advantage of you; learn to see the difference. If you are the one who owes money to your friends, family, or parents please sit with them and tell them you will be paying them back a little bit at a time and write them some cheques. Even if it is only $25 to $50 per month, they will appreciate the effort for their kindness and generosity.

Your Allowance:

This is where we are going to change your bad habits. (But only if you want to!) With the above calculation, you now know where your money is going and how to control it. (You can stop here.) However if you want more out of life with lots of fun and financial security, read on. Basically the more you want, the harder you'll have to work at it, but it becomes easier as you adjust.

The Sacrifices:

This is where you have to have an open mind. We're going to change our little pleasures that cost money and start doing things that are free. Instead of going to a movie, watch one on TV, invite friends over, make a dinner at home with candles, go for walks. I would enjoy walking in higher priced subdivisions for inspiration and would say "I want to live in a nice home like that someday." Well, six years later that's where I lived.

The sacrifices we're going to make are only for a short time (for me it was three years), then it became a way of life that is very rewarding. The first four months of my budget I saved $2000 by just living below my means. I didn't go to or rent any movies, never ate out, watched a lot of TV, and went for walks, biking, and drives. I also did without buying a lot of things. If I needed something that I could live without I would wait until Christmas and put it on my list. The best way I found was to sacrifice from the months of September to April. I would sacrifice eating out and spending money on unnecessary things, but May to August, I would not hesitate and do whatever I wanted because I knew I had sacrificed for eight months. By then, my boyfriend and I had grown out of the habit of going out and shopping, so we ended up still saving money in the summer. What we did was take a trip about 250 miles away, stayed at a hotel, and did some shopping for things we needed and didn't get for Christmas. We also ate out, so that made it a fun getaway. Not shopping at home all year gave us the chance to enjoy a shopping trip.

What I like about saving and cutting back in the months of September to April is that when you come home from work on an April day with the sun shining and the smell of the spring air. You get spring fever. I like to do something, like go out to eat, go biking or for a drive, get an ice cream, but you don't have to feel guilty because you cut back all winter.

Because we broke out of our bad habits and we were saving a lot of money, we created new goals that we wanted to reach. I was 25 years old when I started, I sacrificed for 3 years, and I wanted to be a millionaire at 40 (was that too unrealistic?), I reached my goal at 38 years old. This is where you determine your goals for the future. Everyone's goals are different. You write down the important things to you in life that you want to achieve. For example, you may only want to buy one certain thing, so you may only sacrifice one or two months to save enough money to buy your big TV. That's O.K. because at least you paid cash for something you wanted. Now you may want something else or something more expensive the next time, so you would sacrifice a few more months. If you have bigger goals like a pool or furniture, that would take longer. Some people may have even bigger goals like a cottage, a boat, or a trailer. This is very important. You realize how it works now; if you have less expensive goals, your sacrifices will take less time. I would like everyone to look years ahead and write down your future wish list starting at the end. Where do you want to be at retirement? What kind of stuff do you want to do, and does your partner want the same things? That's why you have to start preparing now. For example, (in my new relationship,), he and I have the same dreams: to live by the water. We both don't like to travel, and I have done my share. The town that I moved to has wooded waterfront lots on the St. John River system with 92 klm of water. When we met, he showed me some land by the water. He said his dream was to build and retire there. I had a cottage on the Northumberland Strait, with salt water and beaches, and my dream was to retire by the water. Once I saw the waterfront lots, in the woods, I loved them. I had a home equity line. I purchased a 1-acre waterfront lot, and he also purchased a 1-acre waterfront lot beside me. We are in our late 40's, and we will have time to pay for it before we retire. With the rising prices of waterfront properties, it is best to try to purchase them as early as possible.

Then we started working on the land on weekends; we love it there all year round. We do some snow shoeing, skiing on the frozen water, making a rink on the ice; he upgraded his boat, and we have family and friends come boating. We purchased a travel trailer to put on the lot and stay there during the summer. We are only 30 minutes from our hometown of Fredericton, NB. I decided to sell my seaside cottage because I wasn't using it. I was renting it, which is good, but I lived 2 hours away and my family had to help take care of it. The value had doubled in ten years.

We're working all the time for our future; we will sell our home and build on the waterfront lot someday. We will reduce our spending by living off the land with a garden and a wood stove. I have friends that want the same things, but they are not doing anything to get there. It is so important to get the most out of your life. *If you don't know where you're going, then how can you get there?* Start saving and plan for your future. Now take charge and make it happen!

A Success Story: A few years ago I was talking to a married couple who had good incomes but didn't know anything about how to budget; all their money would be spent by their next pay. They thought they couldn't afford anything; they sold their second car to help pay some bills. I showed them my budget, but they didn't put it into action. Two years later, they were in the same situation. Their account was in the red (-), and they owed on their credit cards. They saw what I had accomplished in two years, and we talked again about my budget. A month later they told me they had followed my suggestions, and they had paid off all their credit cards and brought their account in the black (+) by one thousand dollars. They had created an allowance for each week and they weren't even spending it; therefore, they were saving even more money. When they saw how much they could save, they didn't feel like spending anymore. Their goals were to travel and to purchase a summer residence. Good going! Update: They purchased a travel trailer to put on his father's waterfront property, and they have re-designed and updated their home. Now they take up to three trips a year to Aruba and other places. They were making twice as much the money as us, but they were spending everything.

Yes I know what you're going to say "We have children" and "We can't save". If your income was 10% less, you would still survive. So think of your children and build up your savings so you can better your future for your family.

Life Story: This person (Joe) had been through bank-ruptcy and had no credit cards. Joe paid cash for everything. While talking with Joe, I said that even if you think you have no money, you are actually in a better place than some of my friends. They have thousands of dollars in credit card bills and end up working but really only trying to pay their past debts. In other words, they would have to work years to back pay their debts from the past. Now the bankrupt person (Joe) has no money but also has no debts to worry about. At lease Joe was spending exactly what money he had. It must be hard to imagine someone not having to live with any credit.

Bankruptcy looks good on the outside (no debts), but it is very hard to live after bankruptcy.

Most people are only 3 to 4 pay cheques away for being homeless...

This is a guideline for you to follow, especially if you haven't purchased a home yet. Do your calculations before you buy!

The breakdown of your income should be:

- House (mortgage): 35%
- Transportation: 15%
- Saving: 10%
- Life: 25%
- Debt repayment: 15%

Denise's Budgeting Tips:
- Buy on sale in bulk items such as bathroom tissue, paper towels.
- Buy one get one free at the grocery store; fill up on those items that you use.
- Put a dollar a day away in a can that you cannot open for five years for a total of $1825.
- Think before you buy something, do I really need it?
- Try to make things yourself instead of buying. Example: beer and wine, cards, food, and Christmas gifts (at Christmas I fill up my house with outdoor cedars tree branches, then you can just throw them out at the end of Christmas...Martha Stewart has great ideas in her magazines.).
- Whenever you purchase your first home try to make it a rental income. Don't purchase a dream home first; you will be poor from paying your mortgage for years.
- Write down your goals for the future and start working on them.

Chapter 2

Looking at retirement

I wanted financial security after seeing my parents still making house payments after 25 years and living from pay to pay. I didn't want to live that way. I knew that in my 20's people didn't normally have lots of money because they were just starting out or have school debts. But then in their 30's people want to have more fun, a home, nice cars, and maybe children, or to travel. You would need more money at this age, but most people don't have any money and they're just adding debt to credit cards. People in their 30's want to live more in the now and not think of tomorrow. So the more you save earlier in life, the better lifestyle you will have later on. Once people are in their 40's they may want to socialize more because the children are older and the parents want to follow their friends with their toys. This is the age people want money, believe me. When all your friends are buying 4 wheelers, skidoos, boats, traveling… you don't want to miss out on the fun. But we seem to accumulate more debt earlier in life. If people are going to follow the children's events and their wants and needs, this can be expensive. The children are already brought up wanting and needing everything they see or their friends have. And the worst of this is, no one will remember or care if your child had everything.

You will want to live a little in your late 40's and 50's because you see the 60's are coming fast, and you might want to be fulfilling more of your dreams. You will want to do your hobbies, like boating, fishing, camping, traveling, etc. So now you get into a panic mode and want to do stuff, but it's going to cost money. You don't want to build up more debts just before retiring. You should now be in a bigger saving mode for retirement. Also you want to still have a great retirement life with no debts, but you keep spending on little things all your life or you are 'lost in life' with no goals or focus. This has happened to me a couple of times in my life, and I have to keep reminding myself to stop, make a budget, and keep on track. I know it's very hard. But then life just goes by, and it is only when you get close to 50 that you realize while thinking back and forward all those questions you ask yourself: Have I enjoyed my life to fullest, or have I just sat there and let life come to me? Was I paying everybody else money and not paying myself? So please everyone just get one thing out of this book: PAY YOURSELF ALSO, SO YOU CAN LIVE YOUR LIFE THE WAY YOU WANT and not the way life is given to you. I want you to make your life your dreams and wants. Just because you might not have had money growing up, doesn't mean you need to live life thinking you can't have your dreams. Everyone can change and also change your life circumstances, you just need to get guidance on how to do it and have the will to do it.

How It Works:

Take the allowance you didn't spend each week, the left-over grocery money, and your savings; remember every dollar is so important. If you can put it in a tax free savings account (TFSA) or guaranteed income certificate (GIC) or registered retirement savings plan (RRSP) for your future, it will work for you.

I would have a suitcase under my bed and put every extra dollar from my allowance in it. Then I would sit there and count all the money to see if I could make $100 dollars. Once all the hundreds added up to 10, in other words $1000 dollars, I would put it in the bank and watch it grow. Remember the POWER OF TEN, $10 x 10= $100 x 10= $1000 x 10 = $10,000. Yes, this is really so exciting to me. Maybe I should stop and say this; every time you save even the smallest amounts it adds up. The process of seeing your money grow will excite you, well hopefully, or it might only be me! Oh well. Let me tell you something you may not have heard before, "**It takes money to make money**". I know, I know, you've never heard this before. That's why I'm telling you. Well, that is how some people become millionaires. It's never too late to start. I mean it.

Millionaire:

Do you want to be a millionaire or multimillionaire? Well anyone can have a MILLION DOLLARS if they want to at retirement. The younger you start, the easier it will be; just save a little bit of money per month for a few years then stop. And think that the magic of compound interest will do the work for you. I think some people don't realize that your money works for you also, you don't have to do all the hard labor all the time. Your money doubles every 14 years at 5% return.

For an example, at 30 years old if you want to be a millionaire at retirement, you would need to save $650.00 per month in an interest paying account of 5% with compound inflation of 3%. You would add 3% to your payment every year. At 65 years old, you would have $1,082,507.

Here is a sample of two different ways to get to 1 million starting at the age of 20 with 5% interest. (You can go to your bank and get this formula for your age.)

If you put $550 per month at 5%, you would end up with $1,083,040 at age 65.

This means you physically put $297,000 of your money, and the rest was compounded for growth.

Or if you start with $325 per month at 20 years old and add 3% to your payment every year, you would get $1,042,635 at age 65.

Example: year 1 – payment of $325 per month, year 2 – payment of $ 335 per month, year 3 – payment of $ 345 per month. By age 38, you would be at $ 553 per month and so on, and by age 50 you would be at $789, and at 60 at $1060 per month for that year. So in this case you would have physically put $361,632 of your money, and the rest would be compound interest.

So the more money you put down at a younger age, the faster and more money for you at retirement. You could have more than 1 million dollars. Also, less of your own money would be used. For the example above, with $550 at age 20 you would save $64,632 compared to the $325 with growth.

I would try to start at $550 per month so it is automatic, and you don't have to think about it. But you make the choice that is best for you. Now if this is too much money for you, then I would like to see even the smallest amount that you can afford to start, then increase as soon as possible.

Remember if you have 1 million in your account and withdraw even 3 to 4 %, you would receive $30,000 to $40,000 per year. That could be the interest alone, without touching the capital (1 million). And if you have children, in your will, have only the interest go to them and keep the principal. This can go on forever for your children's children, only removing the interest not the capital. And as the interest rate goes higher, so does your income.

Now that is one way. However, now there is another way to make money that has great benefits but includes hard work and discipline. If you're willing to get involved with this project, then see Rental Income in chapter 4.

Registered Retirement Savings Plan (RRSP): People didn't talk about them years ago; our parents or schools didn't teach them to us. I meet a lot of people that don't have any RRSP, TFSA, or for the USA 401(K) or don't know what they are! Most people are left only with the money from the government or hopefully the money from the sale of their home to live on at retirement. But wait, you have to live somewhere, and do you need to sell your house to get some money to retire? What if you love your home and you're still in great shape at 65 (or the new retirement age of 67), then what? Sure, if you had a home line on your house then you can use that money, but you're still going to pay interest on your loan, taking money from your retirement to pay the interest.

Well, that's why we need to realize that every day you're living your life, **you need to pay yourself also**. Look at it as a retirement payment. I mean you pay the insurance guy, TV/cable guy, phone bills, car payment, etc. You need to pay the retirement guy too, "YOU". You need to set up a withdrawal or do a onetime payment to "the Retirement Guy", you know, YOU!

What are RRSP and TFSA?

To make this simple, when you purchase a registered retirement savings plan (RRSP) investment from your bank or broker, you are purchasing a product that can have from high risk to no risk; playing the stock market (mutual funds) can be a higher risk. (Your banker can provide more details to better serve your needs), or you can choose a GIC (RRSP) investment where the interest is guaranteed, will not change, and usually is lower with no risk to your investment. Mutual funds can have a higher risk, which means your money will change with the world markets and economy. You can lose the money that you put into your funds. But also you could make a lot more money in a mutual fund than your investment in a GIC. This all depends on your situation and age; if you are younger, the market can bounce back if there is a loss of some capital because of time being on your side. But if you're older, you may choose not to take any risk, therefore choosing a safer investment. When purchasing a RRSP, for example, for $1000, you get your tax money back from the government. If your wages (total gross income) at the end of the year is $41,000 before taxes (gross) or less, your tax bracket, as of 2013, was 24.1%; you would get back *$240.00 for each $1000 you put into RRSP.* If your salary is higher, from $41,001 to $83,000, your tax bracket was 34.1% as of 2013, so you would receive for every $1000 you purchase $340 back. If you would make $41,000 or more, it is better to purchase RRSP because you're in a higher tax bracket. When you are about to cash them, you must pay the government some taxes, so you should be in a lower tax bracket to pay less money.

What if you don't want to be in a lower tax bracket when you retire? You know this book is showing you how to be rich. Always think of your life situation, your goals, and what you're doing at the time to choose the right options. Make the best decisions for yourself. Because with the magic of compound interest, your $1000 has now grown to $10,000. You will have to pay the government the tax percentage of whatever income bracket you're in when you cash the RRSP. Are you confused yet...? So in other words, you have received $340 from your initial $1000, but if you are in the same tax bracket of 34%, you will be paying the government $3400 on your $10,000 growth when you cash it.

But with the new TFSA that I love, which started in 2009, you are allowed to purchase up to $5000 per year for every year since 2009 to put into the account. So if it is 2013, you would have accumulated or are allowed up to $25,500 in total in a TFSA because in 2013 you were allowed $5500. You can purchase the exact same product as an RRSP, the same type of GIC and mutual funds. Or you can just put it in a savings, which would have a lower interest rate, of course. But you don't get any refund money back on your taxes when you purchase them. When your money reaches $10,000 in growth, years from now, you will get ALL the money back without penalty, all yours tax free! You can remove it from the fund at any time, with no penalty; these are not locked in, which I like.

But if you are in a higher tax bracket, or you owe the government some money because you may have had a sale of a property with capital gain, then it can be good to get some RRSP's. You will be getting a higher return, and hopefully if you get a lower wage anytime you can cash them. (However, I still like the TFSA; the only downfall is you are limited to only a certain amount of money. The experts in RRSP really find the RRSP a better deal.)

If possible try to cash your RRSP anytime you are in a lower income tax bracket. If the amount of your RRSP and your gross income added together go over $41,000, then you will pay a higher tax. The faster you remove your RRSP's, (not advised by too many bankers or investors,) the less tax you will pay, but only if you are going to be really disciplined and put this money in the same investment funds that you just removed them from (mutual or GIC funs), but into a non RRSP. It is important to keep the money you have cashed for your retirement. The only difference is, as your funds grow and you are ready to remove them, you will not have to pay taxes on the growth. You may pay some taxes every year on the interest only, but you will get all of the growth of your funds. Top up your TFSA.

In other words, you will pay taxes on a smaller amount if they are removed earlier than if you would have let them grow in the RRSP.

You cannot cash an RRSP that is locked in, which may come from your work; the locked in funds can only be retrieved at retirement. If your company matches your contribution, this is really good, and you should maximize your contribution from work.

A GIC can be locked in for a certain amount of years, with the guarantee of the principle money and the interest. But this will generate a T5 at the end of the year. This is a tax certificate with which you have to claim the interest charge on the interest made. A GIC or Mutual Fund inside the new TFSA grows totally tax free. When you put your money in a TFSA, you do not pay any taxes, even when you remove it.

A RRSP has a maturing time. On Dec. 31 in the year you turn 71 years old, you must make a decision on what to do with your RRSP's. You have three choices:

1. Cash them, but you will be paying full taxes on the total all at once. Depending on how much you will be cashing over $40,000 the tax percentage goes up.

2. Transfer them to a registered retirement income fund (RRIF). An RRIF is an account designed to provide individuals with a source of income after they have retired. It was rolled over so it is still taxable upon removal, and the Canada Revenue Agency prescribes an annual minimum withdrawal amount, which depends on your age and the market value of the RRIF at the beginning of the year. There is no maximum that you can withdraw.

   (In other words you can get a certain amount of money per month. There is a minimum required amount per month, but you can increase it. You can decide how fast the funds will run out. You will pay the taxes on the total you removed at the end of that year; for example, if you want to remove $500 per month, they will tax you on $6000 at the end of the year)

3. Purchase an annuity: The annuity provider makes regular payments (typically monthly) back to the annuity holder. There are two main types of annuity contracts. People can purchase a term that pays them a certain amount of income over a specified period of time or until a certain age. Terms allow the investor to know with certainty the payment period and amount, along with the frequency. If the person dies before the contract is over, the beneficiary will continue to receive the payments, to the end of the stated contract term. ie: 5 years, 10 years. Life annuities provide the beneficiary with a guaranteed

regular income for the rest of his or her life, no matter how long he or she lives. A life annuity can be purchased for a single life or as a joint and survivor life, which is based on the lives of two people. But the beneficiary has no access to the capital. Once purchased, the beneficiary gets income but no access to his or her personal investment. But if the beneficiary is still not sure which way, he or she can do both, purchase an annuity to have guaranteed income and transfer some RRSP into an RRIF for capital growth potential.

The experts will let you know what is best for you at your age and your situation.

Here is the chart for 2013 tax % you pay or receive on your income or RRSP. (Please check your province tax chart)

For $10,000–$41,000 thousand dollars in total gross income, you pay 24.1% in taxes.

For $41,000–$83,000, you pay 34.1%.

For $83,000–$128,000, you pay 38.4%.

For $128,000 and up, you pay 43.3%.

A *Quick Repeat:*

When you put $1000 in an RRSP and receive a minimum $240 back from the government at purchase (at the lowest tax bracket) then years go by, and let's say you're 65 years old and the RRSP is now $10,000 or so, if you were in a lower tax bracket and cashed your RRSP, you would owe the government $2400. Or you can purchase a TFSA for $1000, but you don't get any money back when you purchase it. But when you are 65 years old and you want to cash it, you get all the $10,000 tax free to you. Also today the lower tax bracket is now

24.1%, but that could change in the future; it may get higher. So, if possible, fill up your TFSA. You should start today, I mean TODAY. Call your bank and have them put at least $100 or whatever you can afford go into a TFSA every month……….. hum hum……hum hum….hum …hum… I'm waiting until you get back from your phone call…So how did it go? Good. I am sure you're going to feel good and sleep better knowing you have money building up for retirement.

I KNOW I hear it all the time. "Blah blah, what if I don't live that long?" Oh how many times I've heard, "Enjoy today; who cares about tomorrow?" Well if you died today yes it wouldn't matter if you had money, but what if you LIVE, then what? I say WHAT IF YOU LIVE until tomorrow and maybe even until retirement. You would really want to be ready and not live at a shelter or a food bank because OLD AGE INCOME isn't a lot of money; it's like government assistance (not much) at 65 (or 67) years old. It is about $500 per month (approx.) for old age. And, if you are lucky and get CPP at about $100 to 1000 per month. That's if you worked at least 10 years paying into CPP. How far do you think you can survive with paying for rent, car, and food, never mind your retirement fun time? If you don't have your own retirement money, kiss fun and travelling good bye! You should average $1400.00 per month with government supplement.

Try it then, an exercise of life, take only $1500 cash and make a chart:

INCOME $1500: Remember you may be on your own if your spouse dies.

Let's deduct the amount of money you would need to survive on your own.

If you think your home would be paid for, you need to put money away for repairs.

And if you think you would move out to a rental building then write down your rent, $700-$900. Don't forget you need to add these amounts when applicable: heat and lights, insurance, property taxes, water, snow removal, car expenses, lease payment for vehicle, tires, gas, car insurance, and plates. Then add your essentials, such as food, medical, and clothes. Now how much money do you have left for your nice trip to Florida?

So let's all try to get to our retirement in great financial shape!

Chapter 3

20's, and up....
Read all ages, there is good
information for all.

25 and under

You're looking good, so hey who needs money; you look fabulous. You certainly don't need to shop for beauty stuff you're in your 20's; no wrinkles, tight skin, beautiful (no grey hum hum), hair all naturally silky and shiny, great teeth. You can live in jeans and t-shirts, and no one would notice. Heck you would look great in jeans and t-shirts, men and women. So you don't need to spend any money; how lucky are you! You are at the perfect age to save, save, save, and be poor. Yes SORRY, these are the struggling years; you'll thank me later.

Now there are two roads here you can choose for your life:

SCHOOL if you have chosen to better your life and continue to higher education you will be saying "I really don't have money". You will be studying, and if you're lucky enough to get a part time job or full time summer job, this will help in any way possible to pay your schooling debt. This will be your full focus, but also you can pay yourself a small amount for savings, even if it is only $10.00 per week or less. In four years you'll have $2000. (Put in a TFSA.) So you can live with a couple of pairs of jeans and tops and some jackets for 4 years; heck, who will care? You know a couple of different scarves can change your look! But I strongly think that your future and where you end up does matter. This education can open many doors, and today you need as many doors as possible. So you need to pay your school debts, and if you're lucky and your parents paid some or all of them, then all you need is to put money in a TSFA a.s.a.p., the earlier the better.

WORK …no you didn't win the lotto because you got a job. Remember your friends are in school paying for an education, so they are living in jeans. So guess what, this is where you can also live in jeans and start saving a.s.a.p. You will be ahead for now, but they may get higher paying jobs in the future. But there is no guarantee that they will do better than you. Many business owners that worked hard can make a really good living, even if they didn't finish school. But the key here is working hard at the bottom, to get to the top. And any course or class you can take outside of your job can help provide better knowledge of what you're doing. Remember your 30's and 40's are where you do not want to be in debt over your head and headed for bankruptcy.

This is an example of hard work and climbing the ladder: if you worked in a bakery as a line worker, but then a foremen job came up and you took it or if you work hard at your job and you then take a management position. With more money and more responsibility maybe you can take courses or training. Then you can become a director of the company and then maybe a partner in a small bakery. That is what happened to one of my friends. He now works as a director in a bakery with close to $200,000 in salary. You can do anything if you want it bad enough.

I heard a story that this child had grown up really poor and was made fun of, so his drive to succeed was very strong. He worked hard selling vacuums and other jobs until he started his own business and was very successful. He retired early with millions of dollars. The KEY here is HARD work and determination. I guarantee you it doesn't come easy or come knocking at your door; **you need to go get it.** If your family has money and gives you a better chance, don't take it for granted just because your parents or ancestors made it. You may need to run the business on your own someday. You need to work hard or it could fail.

Medical

You should apply for your own medical plan today, the younger the better. If you get a job with medical, then you can put yours on hold; the charges are about $20.00 per month to keep your coverage. If you change jobs or go self-employed, you can activate your personal plan again. It will continue and not start over at a higher price and not lose any prescription coverage. And don't forget, when you retire your work plan can end also. You will be very happy to have had yours at a lower price with all the coverage…**A MUST DO.**

26 to 35 years old

Well this is where I started, so if you're younger you have that advantage. I didn't continue to study after high school. (It is really important to finish high school.) I wasn't a person with high grades, but my sister and brother really did great in school and moved on to university. So maybe that is why I needed to do well. If you go to university, you're hopefully going to have a better life (but only if you apply yourself). I started working right after high school; I got a job doing office work. At my work they had Canada Saving Bonds; a bond is like a saving account but on paper. So I purchased some each year. CSB are different now. Today they go directly to the bank. Before you used to receive a piece of paper, the bond doubles in so many years (6 - 12) depending on the interest. With bonds you cannot get any more interest after a specific date written on the bond. So you need to cash them. You can only buy these once a year in November for a couple of weeks.

If I were to do it again I would purchase more rental income properties. I only started at 28 with my first duplex, which I still own today, and it has since doubled in value. But my boyfriend was going from job to job, and we talked about owing our own business. We found this little business for sale; it wasn't making any money but was only about two years old. I took my bonds for a down payment on the business, and I kept working full time. He worked at the business behind the counter, and I helped him with marketing and accounting. I learned how to do the bookkeeping with the help of my friend who had taken a course in accounting. The business that we purchased (a beer and wine making store) wasn't making any money, but we had it in us to work hard to make it succeed. As of today the business is very successful.

My boyfriend and I started going out when we were 18 years old, and by the age of 25 we had purchased our business. My parents had just renovated their home and left the basement unfinished. Since my brother and sister were off to university, we decided to finish the basement and move in. It took us a year. We paid cash for our supplies and finished the basement as an apartment. We paid my parents a small rent for heat/power and cable. We had paid for all the materials. Later after we moved out, it was an income for them and an increase in home value. After we had purchased the business, the owner of the property that our business was in wanted to sell the property. We needed to buy it, so we borrowed the down payment from the bank, we took over the existing mortgage on the house, and the owner held a second mortgage.

Now with all this debt, we had a hard time paying the bills. So that's when I started "The Budget". I sacrificed 3 years of no spending. I thought I wasn't spending before, but when I really buckled down I saw even more of a difference. So to recap at 25 we purchased a business, with property, did my budget (from the first chapter), then we purchased a duplex at 28. The next year we purchased a cottage (rented it out), and the money wasn't coming from the profit of the business. My boyfriend had a very small salary, and I had a full time job. We just sacrificed. We saved $40,000 in three years and purchased our dream home in a very nice subdivision, and a few toys like trucks, a sport car, and a jet ski. We stayed in the apartment for 6 years.

The best move I had ever made was to sacrifice during these years because no one really has money at this age. You should put some money away for whatever your dreams are, such as traveling or purchasing your sports car.

Save your money so you can enjoy life and make your dreams come true.

These are the best years to save some money while you are young. Spend some (not a lot) of money. Enjoy your early thirties; you know, you still look fabulous. With the rental income and cottage income you can enjoy your life a little more.

WILLS: If you have children or own a home or have any kind of debt, you should be getting a will. With an appointed person for power of attorney, which means if you are still alive but cannot pay your bills, because of sustaining an injury or being in a coma, you would appoint someone to take care of your finances. You can purchase will kits at local stationary store, fill them out, and bring them to your lawyer or have a lawyer make one up. It may cost a couple of hundred dollars, but you will be protecting all your family and the things that need to be taken care of.

36 to 45 years old

At one point I was purchasing a property every year, and then the banks got more and more strict with the rules of purchasing. By this time I had completed about 15 real estate transactions, purchasing or selling properties (mostly buying). I'm not a big fan of travelling, but I have travelled enough to have seen a lot of places. I lived in England for almost a year (Doncaster). I've changed boyfriends a couple of times; I have no children but am a godmother to three children.

Now at this age you should be looking at your life and ask yourself some questions, such as "Where am I?", "How did I get here?" and "Where is here?" "Is it where I thought I would be?", "Have I done what I wanted to do in life?" During my sacrificing years I made goals as to where I wanted to be at 40, one of which was to be a millionaire, of course. Did that sound too dreamy or greedy?

Well, reach for the top; what is wrong with the highest goals possible? If you added all my properties' worths at market value minus all my debts owed like mortgages and cars, etc., I had $1.3 million at age 38 and owed $300,000. So, yes I did reach my goal, $1 MILLION at age 38.

I'm always counting my net worth, but it seems to change a lot because my situation keeps changing. My boyfriend and I had broken up. We were going out for 18 years, and we had never got married. I feel like Oprah; I never married; I never got my ears pierced. Oops, off topic. Because of the break up, I had to divide everything in half and keep going. But I realized that after the age of 40, I had not created any new goals for myself. I guess I was on a "goal break." Now at 48, I want to create lots of new goals. Writing this book is one of them.

If you always wanted to have a million dollars, then you should take advantage of purchasing properties. The value is always going to go up if you keep it long enough and make sure you purchase them in the right location. Or you can purchase some Mutual Funds and let the compound interest do the work.

Once you've reached your 40's, if you haven't organized your life or finances yet, it is not too late. You should stop and look at where you want to be at retirement and get on that path, now!

Make sure you start your tax free savings account, or RRSP. This is the most important time to plan your future and start working on making your dreams come true.

46 to 55 years old

This is where I am today, 2014. Now you must really listen to what I am about to say. If you ever start to have available cash, either with your saving or in a home equity lines, you need to be really sure when you purchase something, always think ahead. You will probably look at all the positive, fun, and exciting reasons on why you want this specific thing. But also you need to think of the logical reasons; does this purchase really make sense for us? Will we really use it? Does it fit our lifestyle? Because I've seen so many people around this age that have a little bit of equity start purchasing things impulsively, then two months or two years later they realize that it wasn't a good purchase. For example, I will use me first and then my friends …ha-ha… My boyfriend purchased a piece of land on the water, and then I purchased the one beside his. But at the time we just wanted more land side by side. They were both one acre lots. The land next to mine was up for sale, and we jumped on it immediately. We purchased this 2 acres to have more privacy and more land to potentially sell in the future. The price of waterfront keeps rising in value, and we could have placed a cabin there as a rental property. It is perfect for kayaking and for children to be in a private cove. But then we saw another piece of land down the street with 5 acres with really nice waterfront. I purchased that lot in two days. The other three lots were for sale. You almost need to purchase vacant land with a home line because the banks don't easily give money to people for vacant land. I really shouldn't have purchased the 2 acres, but having money gave me what I wanted when I wanted it. You cannot foresee the future so you deal with it, but having the money got me my dream lot, the 5 acres on the water. And that was worth it.

Now here is my friend's example: His wife's parents had a trailer about 2 hours away, and she said she wanted to buy land nearby. So they purchased 2 lots on the water and then installed a septic field. They never got a chance to go use the land so it just remained vacant; they had paid off the property in four years but never used the land. Now that the property is paid, and it's 4 years later, it is for sale. What three things they could have done to make money?

Pausing ... . Pausing.......................So did you think of anything that they could have done to make money or better use of the land?

  A. If they weren't going to use the land and it had a septic on it, they could have rented it out to trailers for the summer. You could get about $1500 per year x 2 lots. So $3000 per year x 4 years = $12,000 made on land. (He's going to kill me when he reads this.)

  B. Do not pay the land off and only do your minimum payments, then invest your money in a rental property. If the rental income produces money after expenses, it could have probably made the payments of the land, so free land. In other words, the renters are paying for the property and the land. Do you see how your money can work for you? This is how you get rich.

  C. If they would have noticed sooner that they were not using the land, maybe after two years they could have sold it.

In this age group I find a lot of women don't want to work anymore. Yes, they kind of like their job, but they've been there for years and it's the same old same old. When they take a vacation maybe 3 or 4 weeks in a row, well there are a lot of sad faces going back to work. And they are counting the years until they retire. They're thinking, if I wouldn't use my car to work and wouldn't have to buy fancy clothes all the time, look at all that money I would be saving if I wasn't working. The women that age are thinking, honey, can you find a part time job outside your full time job? I wouldn't mind if I didn't see you on Saturdays. I'll be at the cottage. If you see your wife pick up a calculator and you know she's not balancing her cheque book, she's adding how much money she could live without and when she could quit her job and stay home. Heck, she could start making homemade bread, pies, and jams, pickling, even planting a garden. This would save money. If she didn't have to work, she could have time to take care of a garden! So just hang in there ladies and start preparing your lifestyle for retirement.

Around your late 40's early 50's you're starting to get tired of getting up early for work, getting ready in snow storms (for some of us). I wanted to make sure I was going to be at a point at this age that I could have a choice to quit work or work part time at a job I love. And it's been two years that I work only 32 hours per week. I have Monday morning off, Friday afternoon off, and start at 9:00 am the rest of the week. I can go walk the dog in the morning, do some housework or shopping before work. I love my job (assistant to a realtor), and I could do this work past 60, even cutting back to 3 days a week. If you work full time and don't like your job, try to look at finding a full or part time job (whatever money you need to survive) that you like and could maybe work less hours in the future rather than being in a job you don't like for the rest of your working years and then retiring. You must enjoy your life today before you wake up and you're too old to start living.

Retiring at 55 was all the rage when I was younger, but now that we are there it's not that easy and life is too expensive to do that. That Freedom at 55 is now, " When will I have freedom?"

Rental Income: If you're thinking of a rental income at this age, it's still OK. I'm still looking at purchasing some more income properties too. The difference now is that your property that you purchase should bring in some money for you after expenses. If you had more time and if you were younger, it wouldn't matter as much because you don't care if it brings in profit after expenses since it's long term. But now it's not for the long term; it's for now to bring in more money. You know maybe your wife may want to leave her job early, and you don't really want to work on Saturdays. You can buy a rental that will bring in some money. The best way, if you can, is putting down as much as possible, so the mortgage payment won't be so high, take it for the most years possible, so you have more income now. Then later you can always sell it (in your sixties) or leave it for to your children.

56 to 64 years old

Well, I'm not there yet, but these are the critical years before your retirement. At 60 you can apply for the Canada Pension Plan (CPP) (if you worked and contributed into CPP), or wait and collect it to get more money per month at 65, but not much more. I would collect now.

You can still work after collecting CPP, and the government will deduct CPP on your stub, but the next year you will get an adjustment on your CPP income to a bit more. But at age 65 you can optionally keep paying into CPP, or not.

WHAT HAPPENED TO FREEDOM 55? Did any of you get insurance to retire at 55? Many government workers take the early retirement package at 52 or 55 and then get really bored waiting for their spouses to retire for 10 years. You know you can't golf in the winter. And you do realize you'll be home cooking supper and doing the laundry.

If you get one lump sum you could invest into rentals to increase your cash flow. If not, you can invest in mutual funds or TFSA.

But if you are both retired, hopefully you have been saving and can enjoy your future retirement because living on an old age pension isn't going to be nice.

If you think you're OK with a company pension, just listen to these stories.

This worker had money going into a **company** pension; when I say company, I mean his employer was taking the money off his pay, maybe matching some, but it would stay within the company and not transfer to a financial institution in his name.

Just one year before he was about to retire, the company went into receivership (before bankruptcy). The company used some of their pension money, not leaving it there for the retirees. Luckily they were taken over by another company. In the end when he retired, he lost 30% of his retirement money.

Most companies transfer money to a financial Institution with your name on it, and you would receive a statement from which you could see your investment. But if it stays in the company name, there is always a risk that the company may spend it or go bankrupt.

IT IS SO IMPORTANT that you take care of yourself and also save for retirement because you never know and should not count on others for your money.

Another case: This company had a retirement plan, and then the union came in and introduced another plan. They all voted for it and ended up with a very bad plan. Some people lost a lot of money per month by changing plans. Some employees brought them to court, paying lawyer fees for over a year fighting them, but only got a few changes made to their plan. At retirement they would be paying so many fees that they wouldn't receive hardly anything. You see, other people are deciding where your money goes. But you have no choice when you work there, so you just pretend it does not exist. Do your own saving, and if you get something from the company consider it a bonus.

65, 67 and up

Wow you're here; you made it. How does it feel? You know everybody is counting the day until they get here. Did you take a hammer to the alarm clock yet?

Looking back, did you do most of all the things you wanted to do with your life, or has it all been saved up for right now? Can you afford your dream retirement? Well, hopefully you will be living out your dream retirement! Some people still work part time to afford to take trips. You really need to do a budget and figure out how much your home and living expenses will be costing you.

If you have a registered retirement savings plan (RRSP) and you're now waiting to cash them, you will be taxed. You can only keep them in an RRSP account until the age of 71 years, and then you need to move them out into a registered retirement income fund (RRIF) account.

Did you check into your medical insurance that you were paying at work to see if it is transferred to your personal name and covers your previous prescriptions? If it doesn't and you are retired, then you need to apply again for medical, with day one starting today. Which means all your previous medication that was covered from your work, will not be covered anymore, only any new prescriptions that starts today!

Now you can apply for your old age pension; it is about $500 per month. It is time to enjoy your days; try to volunteer, take fun classes, and live life to the fullest!

Chapter 4

Rental Income

For People Who Want a More Secure Future

Here you have to build a foundation—the more foundations, the bigger the income. Remember, you need money to make money; that's a fact. Now where did I hear that before? I just showed you how to get money without leaving your job. Now the money you've saved and sacrificed for, you can put it in an income property. You may have thought I would have said *buy a business*; well, only if this is your goal. In buying a business you may have to leave work, and you will be working hard and long hours with no guarantee of success. But you can still keep your job and have your evenings free if you buy an income property. You need about 20% down payment if you're not going to live in it. I always suggest if you're going to purchase your first home, you may have small children or no children then *purchase a rental income first*. The rental income money will help you a lot in life. MAKE THE SACRIFICE and get some sort of income from your home. Then if you need to have more space because your children are getting older, keep the rental and rent both units and then use the equity to purchase your other home.

My Suggestions for an Income Property

I like buying duplexes, split entry or bungalows that are not more than 30 to 60 years old. The price range is good, and they have the look of a house with a basement apartment. With these rental types, the value increases like a home and can be sold and transformed back into a home. If you get something older, especially in the downtown area, they seem to be more run down with lots of problems and need repairs. You would need to charge lower rent because you will be competing with new apartment buildings. The reason I wouldn't buy an apart-ment block or 5 or 6 units (unless it was a retirement building 55 years old or older) is because as they get older and outdated (interior décor), you are competing with the new ones build-ing up each year. You still have to pay for your building for 20 or more years but may have to reduce the rent. People want to move to newer buildings. I really like buying a duplex in a two to five klm area, out of town, in a residential subdivi-sion. I get tenants that stay longer; they have a back yard and a more homey feeling. I'd rather own six duplexes than one 12 unit apartment building. You can always sell one home if you need money. It's harder to sell a big apartment block, you'll probably lose money. Now the side by sides, I never like or believed in them, you should try to avoid owning half of a side by side. Owning both sides is better. That is my motto, but "guess what", I bought a big side by side. However at the time

I got it for a good deal, and it was my uncle's home that he built. It was a beautiful place with lots of land, and I was planning to live in half and rent the other. I fixed it up and have rented it for over a dozen years now. Yes, of course, for a renter and landlord these places rent fast. People don't like to live in a basement apartment. But remember it is easier to sell an up and down split than a side by side. Also, the up and down can be returned or used as a single family home again, keeping the value going up. If you plan on purchasing half of a duplex, you can run into some problems as they get older. What is going to happen when the roof needs fixing; will both parties have the money? In the bigger cities this type of living is very common, and both sides can look very different. Living in one side, you are living very close to your neighbor! You can't kick out bad neighbors if you don't own the other side, if they are loud, or become a problem. You are stuck next to them. So it is better to own both sides. Also with mine, once the value of the home becomes too high, then the income from renting didn't make sense anymore. It cost more to keep it than the value of the return on the dollar. My side by side is for sale, and I will be taking a loss because the value of return is no longer there.

When you buy your first duplex with the money you saved, don't forget YOU saved all that money so you will still save money because your standard of living has changed.

Calculate the income from your rental, minus your expenses, and this equals the money you have left to pay your mortgage. Once that property is paid, then that income belongs to you. If you had three duplexes paid, this would give you a good income. When you realize you don't want to do the up keep anymore, you sell them, and there is your retirement money to live on.

Don't be scared or negative about owning a duplex. People think it's hard work. If you followed my suggestions about buying in good subdivisions and not too old you shouldn't have any problems. What's the worst thing that could happen? The electrical system should be in good condition because it's not an old house; you rent the hot water tank so the company can come to change it for nothing. The plumbing wouldn't be that old. You may get leaky faucets or water problems, so then you call a plumbing company that has 24 hour service. I have my tenants write 6 to 12 month postdated cheques so you don't need to go bother them everymonth. Plus everything you buy for the duplex is tax deductible, even the interest on the mortgage.

Now I'm not saying everything is rosy all the time. The more properties you have, the more things you need to deal with. Things will happen I guarantee, more often things with the renter than with the house. Don't accept pets; they cause more problems, especially dogs. I know, I know I will get slack for that, but hey I'm a dog owner and I love dogs. But you can't have people living together with the dogs barking, and the tenants not picking up the poop. The lawn gets yellow, and the male dogs kills trees. Then the lawn cutting guy is calling you because he has poop all over his lawn mower tires. Sorry dog owners, but I want to deal with the fewest problems that I have to.

Some renters may be late in paying. I tell them that after 5 days they will be charged $5.00 per day late fees, and I get it. Always remember that they are paying your mortgage; as soon as there is money coming in, that will be **your** money someday. And if you're lucky enough you may be collecting some extra money every month after all your bills are paid. When the banks were giving zero money down, I had a harder time finding good people because they were buying houses and not renting. But now with the 5% down and the economy not doing so well, there will be more people that will have to rent. When the economy is bad, buy duplexes or triples. Speaking of multi units, the more people under one roof the more people problems, but you make more money. DON'T get discouraged when something happens. You're going to get through it, and it will get better. You just need to fix it ASAP.

Be a good landlord. Your tenants will respect you better if you can fix the little things ASAP and get them newer things like kitchen and doorknobs upgraded. If they have nicer things they may be happier where they live. I give all my tenants Christmas gifts, wine and chocolate. By updating your rental property you increase the value for resale. I've seen so many houses that have a hard time selling just because of décor; they'll drop the price by 10's of thousands of dollars. But if they would have kept their home up to date throughout the years or even put in a couple of thousand dollars for some upgrades and paint, they would have gotten their appraised value.

You should increase your rent every year by at least 1% plus round off. If you have great tenants and you do not want to increase their rent, tell them you need to keep the rent up to date for the future. Because, if you ever decide to sell and your rent is really low, it doesn't look good for a new buyer seeing low rent. Also, if you are going to the bank to purchase something else then your rental income would look better. But I'm not finished. What I suggest for you to do is, if you have a great tenant, GIVE THEM THE MONEY BACK in cash or gift cards. For example, if the rent is $800 and you increase it to $810, that is $10.00 x 12 months, which is $120 per year, then give them $120 back at the end of the year.

Now if you ever were looking at purchasing or selling rental income properties, there is a formula that some realtors and investors use to calculate what they call the **Cap Rate**. It is finding the current gross or net income multipliers.

The difficulty with this is finding market information for comparable properties for a market price. On the surface, the calculation of cap rates seems to be a relatively simple process. However, it is with difficulty and uncertainty, and requires a lot of digging for information, questioning, and being alert to special circumstances, which may distort the answers.

Rental Income Capitalization Rate: the

Cap Rate is calculated as follows,

Cap Rate: (Net Operating Income/Market Value) x 100

NOI= cash remaining after deducting the operat-

ing expenses from the Gross Income.

Example:

Net Operating Income (NOI): $239,430

Market Value (MV):$3,420,000

Cap Rate= (239,430 / 3,420,000) x 100

Cap Rate= 7%

The cap rate of 7% represents the annual return before mortgage payments and income taxes on the total investment of $ 3,420,000

So if you just had a hard time understanding this, you are not alone. I've tried reading more on this several times and still don't quite get it. I get this formula, but it goes deeper than this, so you can look it up online or talk to professionals that deal with these formulas.

Chapter 4

Please rent for as long as you can; you can save a lot of money. Your rent money would hardly cover power/insurance/water bills in a house. Save your money until you can buy a rental property or two.

Sometimes when you're in a relationship, you may be the saver but your partner isn't or the reverse. It can be hard to be on the same page, especially in a new or second relationship, and when people are carrying other debts. For example, I'm a super saver, but when I get in new relationships, the other person may not be a saver, so I "get lost in life" again. I would spend more money than I would have if I was single. But it's good to have a balance. What fun would I have if I stayed home saving money my whole life? I wouldn't be having too much fun. So it is good to have a little balance.

Chapter 5

Your Foundation

If your goal is to own a summer residence, like a cottage, then buy it in a good location. It can pay for itself by renting it for six weeks a year. That would cover most of your expenses for the year. Also you can spend the rest of the summer, fall, and spring there. When your cottage is paid, then that money is extra to save, and you can keep your cottage for a retirement home. Or, you can sell it and pay off your new house in your *favorite subdivision*. Also, by keeping it and renting it, it could pay for a toy, car, boat, etc., or better yet some duplexes.

Your foundation: purchase your properties in this order:
Duplex, Duplex, cottage, house.

Once these properties are paid, you'll have income for your future.

Start with your duplex as your first home, rent the basement, then depending on your lifestyle or age you can go for the cottage next. Or move into another duplex, then maybe if you need more room for the kids then go for the house.

Remember a cottage or land by the water, lake, or ocean is a great place to bring up kids with family time.

Go see your bank and start by finding out your *credit score,* a score from 1-9, which indicates to the bank how good of a client you can be with your payments. By keeping your score high it will give you great banking leverage. Keeping a high limit on your credit card and owing less than half is better than a low limit and owing everything. Paying your cards and power bill on time will make your score better so you can get the things you want. Now, also check with them if you have any other cards that are open but not being used. That report from the bank will show you all your cards, and then you can call the companies and close unused cards.

If possible I would suggest only one or two credit cards depending on your age. If you're young to middle aged and you're starting a family and own a home (huh hum duplex) I think you should carry maybe two cards, a Visa and a Master Card. If you are Travelers, get one with air miles; if not get one with points. There can be a fee per year on your credit cards, but if you get a points card you will probably get your points turned into (gas, Visa or store cards) that will amount to more than your fee per year.

Now I'm in my late forties and I don't travel, so I'm getting ready for retirement. I have only one credit card with no fees and a $25,000 limit. With every 2 dollars I spend I get a point and I get free gas cards; it also reverses the fees off of my checking account at the bank. So in other words my $7 to $11 fee I would get charged in my checking account for writing cheques is zeroed out. Those are the options with my card. I got it at Royal Bank, but check with your bank for the option that is best for you. My interest charge is high but I pay my card off every month, and I use it for gas and groceries, which helps me to keep track on how much I'm spending each month on those items.

After you have been budgeting for years, you will notice that you will no longer have to count every penny because you will have changed your habits, and most of all, you will be conscious of what you are buying!

Banking

I would suggest being simple with your banking, I've met people that deal with 3 banks and have 3 to 4 different bank accounts; consequently, they don't have a clue what's going on with each account. They are paying 3 times the fees. So make it simple. I recommend dealing with only one bank using one checking account, from which you can write cheques. Have your mortgage deducted and your payroll deposited in this same account, ultimately saving on bank fees. You don't really need a savings account, unless you need to put money away for later, but also you can have money transferred to your TFSA. If that is full, pay your bills.

I'll show you how to write a cheque.

Example:

Write the recipient's name to whom you are paying on the first line. Print the dollar at the end and write the amount of the dollar in full writing. Always sign on the right bottom, and you can put the info that is referred to on the left.

Pay to _____Ella Harrigan_____	$500.20	
Five hundred dollars_____	.20 dollars	
RBC		
Fredericton		
RE:_____Inv# 34_____	per: Denise LeBlanc_____	

With all the cards today, I find lots of people don't know how to write cheques.

Also, some may do online banking, which I'm starting to like a lot. I generally do not find a savings account to be much use if you have debt. Eliminating debt is a higher priority, and if you are debt free, I recommend a TFSA. If you are a good saver and you have reached the limit of your TFSA, then try some guaranteed income certificates (GIC's). You can always keep some money in your checking account; some offer interest if the balance is higher than a certain amount, say $300. Then it is easier to follow one account. Try to simplify your banking; it will help you be better organized in your quest for financial freedom!

Mortgages

Oh! Those dreaded mortgages; they cost so much money in interest. Well, at least the interest is a lot lower than years ago. In 2011 and 2012 there were the lowest rates I've seen, which have ranged from 2 to 5 %. We used to pay 9, 13 and even close to 20% back in the 70's and 80's. But back then savings also made more money. Mortgage debt can sometimes be positive, because the real estate value trends upwards over time. Someone said to me once, "In the US people are losing their homes and it may not be a good time to buy a house/rental." I said, "What do you mean? This is the perfect time to buy rental property. It is less expensive. And because people have to live somewhere, if they can't afford their homes then they will have to rent!" People listen to the news and make assumptions but each province and each town is different. We have booming towns and towns where companies may be closing, which can affect the housing market. Pay attention to what supports the town's economy. THIS IS the time that you need to think like an investor! You will see that once you own one or two rentals and you see the value of your property double in ten years. Thus you should feel great that the renters paid for your property. Also after expenses, you have made a little extra money each month. Then add all of that money. Thus you see the value of owning rentals. Also, you will think differently about owning a rental knowing that people need to live somewhere and you provide that service.

I recommend watching the real estate market and try to understand it. (I listen to bankers and accountants on their advice for the government's laws. They may not have any experience in buying and selling properties. But the bankers know their products, like RRSP's and mortgages.)

OK back to mortgages, you should take the longest amortization possible so you have more money to save and invest. I recommend investing into more properties as early as possible, because every year the rental homes go up in value and you don't want to miss a year. Try to make payments bi-weekly (you make two more payments per year). Even better, take the accelerated payments if possible (an accelerated payment is taking one payment, which they divide by 12 and then add it to your mortgage). This is all about putting more money down on the principle. You can always put about 10% down anytime, or on the anniversary of your mortgage, depending on what bank you use. Now if you have a rental income, your interest on the mortgage is tax deductible. This deduction can even apply to your own home if you have a rental income in your basement, but only in proportion to the percentage of rental space. With interest rates at an all-time low, and a possible tax deduction of the interest payments themselves, it would be better to invest in more properties.

Now let's pause for a moment, and I'm going to talk about your taxes. If you have a rental property, either in your home or separately, you must keep records. You should take a piece of paper and write down the income from your rental each month (one page per unit).

What I do is write the tenants' names with their phone number, whether or not I own the washer and dryer in that rental, and what they paid for a damage deposit. After a few rentals, this makes it easier to keep track.

You need to get a folder to put all of the receipts for your properties to keep all your papers in. I have a folder for each house I own. So all my receipts of the year go in the file, and at the end of the year after I add them up, I put them in a big brown envelope for my accounting.

Add all the expenses minus your rental income, and this becomes your profits that are added to your salary that you will pay taxes on. Remember they don't use your mortgage payment as an expense, only the interest. Now if you live in the home with a rental income, you would claim the things that your tenant would use, power bill, if internet and cable is provided for them, snow removal, water bill, property taxes, and repairs or renovation to the home that reflect their apartment. What you need to determine is the percentage of space your apartment takes in your home. Let's say it's 40% of your home. I have an extra room downstairs on my side, and they have the rest so I have it at 40%, but if they take the whole basement then you could claim 50%. Then take the total of the expenses (bills that you both use, like power) that affect the apartment and calculate 40% or 50% of the expense. Add your rental income then minus your expenses for you to claim on your taxes. Don't forget the interest on your mortgage. Also, don't worry that your income may look larger when paying taxes; remember they are helping you pay the mortgage. The value of your home will increase, which also makes it easier for borrowing more money.

OK now back to mortgages again, once you have paid down some of your mortgage, the value of your house has gone up, and you have over 20% of equity in your home, you can do a home equity line on your property. This will be different depending on which bank you are using. For me I love the one I have with Royal Bank. I've seen others and they are totally different than the one I use at Royal Bank.

Home Line

Let's say your home is appraised at $200,000 for an easy number. Example, (rule may change during the course over the years) the bank would take 80% of the appraised value of your home ($160,000) and give you access to this money on a home equity line. So the debt plus the cash available must equal $160,000. It always needs to balance to $160,000.

If you have an existing mortgage (you can leave it in a mortgage form or leave it all in a home equity line) depending which one is the low interest. For example, if $100,000 is your mortgage to make it easy, so now you have $60,000 cash available to use at any time. Then you transfer your debt to your home line at a lower interest rate. So you can pay off credit cards or car payments because usually the Home Line will be the best interest out there. Today it is 3% for me. They always say to get a mortgage that is *open* because you pay a smaller interest rate, but I've just seen 2.69% locked in for 2 years, so if you're not going to pay your house off or sell it in the next couple of years, I would lock it into a mortgage and keep the rest in a home line.

So again on paper it shows:

160,000 available

-100,000 mortgages

60,000 home line

(It always has to balance to 160,000.)

The balance left available for you is 60 thousand; you can pay off anything that may have a higher interest. For every dollar you owe on this home line the interest is directly removed from your checking account. You would see the interest come out of your account, and you are only working with the $160,000 on the home line. Now if you want to do a payment on this debt, you can ask the bank to do an automatic payment of whatever amount you wish. If you made a $500 dollars per month payment, it would go on your home line to pay on the principle. You can also remove it again at any time.

Also, as your mortgage is being paid, the amount of principle will go on your home line. Every dollar on principle you pay on your mortgage will be added to the home line to add up to $160,000. Are you confused! A lot of people are when you first hear about this, but it's a great thing once you use it. Don't get carried away spending money that you can't pay back. When you sell your home, it pays the total home line.

Now the interest on this home line let's say is 3%, but if it goes up, you could say to the bank you would like to lock in 20k (or whatever big amount you may owe) at the going rate before it goes up. They would lock in the 20k and you would now be making payment on that 20k. With the existing mortgage, and the 20K, you are only allowed to do one other lock in. They only allow 3 times. If your mortgage rate was going to be higher than the home line rate then you could cancel your mortgage and only pay what you want per month when you want to. It saves people that may have had a bad situation and couldn't pay their mortgage, and then you don't have to do any payment at all. The only thing is that the interest will be coming out of your checking account.

Some people who are spenders would look at this as a big opportunity to purchase lots of stuff. Remember you're still being charged interest.

To repeat again, the fun part is that every time your mortgage payment comes out, you have more money available to you. The home line always has to balance to $160,000 so for every payment you make you can go back to get that cash. It is always available to you. Now if you were smart with your money and you have some houses that you can get home lines on, then you have cash to buy other rentals or a cottage or land by the water without going to the bank. All you do is move the money from your home line to your bank account.

Example story:

One of my friends is single, owns a home and works as a laborer (painter), so that means if he gets hurt he can't work. His home is probably worth over $100,000, but he only owes $20,000. I told him about the home line. He went and got one and now he doesn't have to worry about his mortgage payments if he has a bad month from painting. He has $20,000 in a home line with only the interest coming out of his account. This should be less than 100 dollars per month, and then he can put what he can afford on the principle. Also, it allowed him to fix his bathroom and move money to pay off his truck, so no more credit card debt or car payment. He would have access to about $80,000 dollars.

Don't give up if your bank is not too cooperative; if you really want a property, keep trying. You may find other banks to lend you the money. Then later you can always transfer it back to your bank. If my bank refuses me, I get it somewhere else (sometimes the interest may be higher) and after a few years then I go see my bank and they are more than happy to take it. I just like having everything under one roof. When you get older you don't have to remember where all your stuff is. I use to have 3 different mortgages at 3 different banks and I had to write cheques to pay all the different bank payments, so I decided to merge everything under one roof. Simplify your life because owning rental will keep you busy enough.

There are so many different things going on all the time. I keep hearing about different ways to make money in real estate, such as buying a home at 50% of value, which may work in different towns or countries. But once you know your town/city with the prices for homes and situations, it doesn't matter what people are saying; you will have a better idea of the reality of things in your town/city.

TO RECAP,

★ Always purchase a rental property first.

★Get your banking stuff organized.

★Get a home line as soon as you can.

Chapter 6

Business

I think a lot of people have thought about owning their own business. Being your own boss gives you a feeling of freedom. You don't have to live by someone else's rules or have to ask for time off for simple things that just happens in life. If you just need one or two hours during the day to buy a car, go to the dentist, go to the doctor, or go to the bank, you can do it. We always seem to live outside of our working hours; that's our life, and there is not much time left at night or weekend to do everything. Not having that freedom to be somewhere in the middle of the day can be hard. But we all need that pay cheque, and that isn't always a lot of money. You can only live with that guaranteed money that you know is coming on payday. You try to pay your home and car while your family's future is depending on your job, which you may not have control of. And if you get laid off, your world has to change and everything is affected. That is why it is important to put money away for unforeseen things that *can* **happen in life**.

(I really wanted to say that "*will* **happen in life**" because there is a bigger chance something will happen.) I lost my job about 5 times in 25 years because of company changes, offices moving, government changes, and companies being sold. I always have my own RRSP's and insurance because I don't want to be dependent on the government for my retirement. I'm taking care of myself, for my future. Owning property is my way of taking care of my future and having my money work for me while I'm working as well.

Looking at starting a small business!

If you have an idea, a passion or a talent and you wish to start your own business. You must know one really, really IMPORTANT thing. NEVER, NEVER START A BUSINESS FROM SCRATCH IF YOU ARE <u>ONLY</u> INTERESTED IN MAKING MONEY; your mind won't be able to handle the hard work and bad sales days. The last thing you want is to start a new business with the frame of mind of only making money.

I tell anyone who is starting a business, "Never let your emotions control your business." You will have good days, great days, and bad sales days. Don't ride the roller coaster of everyday sales; **work in your business for the love and freedom of being your own boss** and years will go by and you will only need to look at the bottom line of your business. Work on increasing overall sales and marketing your business.

While speaking about bottom lines, if you have to choose an accountant to do your bookkeeping in your business, please make sure you know where you stand at all times.

Check often on how much you spend and how much you make, because you can't make any decisions to purchase something if you don't know if you can afford it. For example, my friends opened a restaurant with inherited money, but they did not watch their spending. They were not good with the accounting, and didn't know where they stood in their business. So even though the business was good, they still needed to close it down due to overspending. You need to have an idea on what is going on and how much you are spending. I always say running a business is like running your personal life, "Same concept, different look."

Starting your own business from zero.

First, of course, you have the idea, (make sure you weighed all the negative and positive of your business) so you don't get surprised later if you run into a problem.

STEP 1–Register the business name; it doesn't have to be a limited company.

STEP 2– Get your payroll and HST number. You do not have to charge HST if your sales are going to be less than $30,000 that year. But do it anyway for the future.

STEP 3–Find a great location for your type of business. Location can break or make a business. It is very important. (Location depends on your target market.)

STEP 4– If you are leasing a property, negotiate a better rate or free rent for half or the first month to get on your feet.

STEP 5–If you're hiring employees, look into government programs. They may pay one employee a portion of their hourly rate for one year, and/or a $10,000 loan. If you are on EI they may pay you another year of EI. There is lots of stuff out there to help small businesses.

Some banks can get you a business Visa before you even open, if you have good credit. You could get up to a $50,000 limit on a business Visa.

STEP 6-When getting your place ready to open, you feel excited and you're making your place look fresh and new. Keep in mind that once you have been in business for a while try to come in with new eyes. I walk into businesses and see that the owners got too comfortable at their store, and it looks like they don't see what other people see coming in (like personal things hanging around the counter or behind the counter but still visible to the clients) . So make your store as nice as possible, and please keep it clean. Wash floors and vacuum front door carpet. This should be done before you open every day.

STEP 7-Wow I bet you didn't realize how much that sign was going to cost you on your building. Yes, advertising is expensive and what you pay in advertising sometimes does not get much of a return. So it is important to find out whom your target market is, what age group, and what they're seeing or reading. Choose these avenues to proceed with marketing carefully. Making business cards and your advertising material should be used at the least cost to you as possible. Starting a new business from the ground up is the hardest thing to do. You spend a lot of money in advertising to bring people there, so make sure once they're in there you wow them.

CUSTOMER SERVICE is the best way to grow your business. This is very important, and you don't realize that the word of mouth is the best advertisement.

In everyday business, you will be spending money on your store signs and material, employee payroll, training time, inventory and suppliers, so maybe there might be some left over money for yourself. Probably not! Because you will feel like you want to put anything left over on your debt. Remember always pay yourself too, even if the company is carrying some debt, as long as you're paying all your suppliers and the important people. Give yourself a little bonus at the end of the year. If you give yourself payroll make it small to start. Remember you are the business, and you will probably owe on credit line debts for a couple of years.

The GOOD and the BAD things about owning a Business.

GOOD

- You're self-employed, and that means freedom.
- Possibility to make more money.
- Company pays your car and phone etc…
- Pride in being a business owner
- Taking time off at your leisure

BAD

- If your company isn't doing well.
- Can't pay yourself.
- Working harder and longer hours than a full time job.
- Not knowing if you have any money at the end of the week.
- Higher level of stress.
- And your business is on your mind 24 hours a day.
- Can't take time off.

Are you still with me to own your own business?

On the other hand, being an employee and having a guaranteed income could be a good thing. You actually know how much money is coming in. While owning a small business, you're not sure if you are going to have any money tomorrow.

Starting a Franchise or Existing Business

Looking to PURCHASE an existing business or purchasing a franchise also has its good and bad sides. When buying an existing business that is run by a sole owner you can run into a problem. The customers are going to this business because of the owner. So if you purchase this business and you are the new face behind the counter, you're not guaranteed to have the same sales that he has built up for years. They may not come back. For the over the counter type business, you can fix a bit of that by being a new face behind the counter for a while with the owner and then the people will get to know you. Then you can announce that you're the new owner later.

If this is a different business and the owner is silent in the business, you may have a greater chance to keep the same or do more business even if the sales are not that good. You can turn it around. (An example of this is a restaurant/bar where the customers see the staff more and come for the food). Now if this was a franchise then the name sells itself. It may have been poorly run by the last owner, and you may do a better job of running it and create better morale for the staff.

If you wanted to purchase a business that may be a couple of years old but not making money, and you have it in you to work hard to make it succeed, know that the first 5 years in business are the hardest. If the previous owners already did the hardest part, which is the first two years, and you have it in you (I stress this because you cannot be lazy and just keep it running), you must want to keep on pushing to get customers.

These people may have just given up on the business and didn't want the hard work.

Example: The business that I purchased was two years old and wasn't making money, so people were saying not to buy it. But we had it in us to make it work. We delivered flyers to mailboxes on Sundays, (not sure if you are allowed to do this today but you can advertise in the local newspaper or in the bag of flyers that go to every household). We did lifestyle (trade) shows. The business was growing every year, and to this day, 23 years later, it is still growing in sales. And the number one reason for this is CUSTOMER SERVICE. This is what makes a big difference in your business. People are paying you; they deserve the best and the friendliest service possible. So purchasing an existing business instead of a franchise is a lot easier to deal with and you have no one to answer to, except your clients.

If you are undecided but want to own a franchise, then get the magazine about the TOP franchises at your local bookstore and read up on the businesses and ideas. Some have ads looking for buyers.

Buyers beware; you can purchase a great name business but never own the building that the business is in. You are just there to make the money, like a middle man. You will most likely pay a franchise fee on your sales and maybe your profits, but they could be a really big franchise and most likely have big sales. So it's like you run it and make good money. Any business that is a franchise you will probably always be connecting to the home company with fees.

So here are your choices:

A. Start from nothing and build up your business with lots of advertising, word of mouth and great CUSTOMER SERVICE.

B. Purchase an existing business young or old and continue to expand it or run it with great CUSTOMER SER-VICE.

C. Purchase a franchise and the name can sell itself, but you always pay fees and give great CUSTOMER SERVICE.

I just read a great story. It's about this guy who weighed 240 lbs. and smoked one and half packs of cigarettes per day. His son wanted him to do a "fun and run" with him. He wondered how fun and run went together! But he ran with his son and was tired, sweaty, bent over in pain, but that somehow changed his whole life. He started running more and it must have inspired him because he opened a business selling running shoes and clothes. He rented a room off of a hair salon, and called it "The Running Room." John Stanton started opening stores that were in competition with big name sport stores, and he was doing great. The reason for his success is he had people who knew about running that worked for him (customer service). With over 100 stores open, he is a great inspiration. Way to go John!

Don't let your dreams die because you think you may not succeed. Thinking outside the box is so important. There are always certain people who are always thinking of something different that would make a great business idea or doing different things in their existing business. Some people just seem to just follow everyone else, not thinking of making any changes to their business or lifestyle. If everyone else is doing this, I'll just follow. For example, if you're a real estate agent, there are probably about a couple of 100 of you in your town. How are you going to stand out? Or are you never going to stand out?

I had someone notice that my business was doing well, so they opened a similar business across town. But even if their business sold identical products to mine, they didn't really know how to run a business. They made big mistakes that cost them money, and they eventually closed. We are always going to make some mistakes. We may try different things in our business, and if they aren't working we need to correct them quickly.

I would like to say GOOD LUCK in your adventures in following your passions. You may start part time until you can support yourself before you quit a job to open your own business.

If you're purchasing a small business, and it really is only the inventory, that's fine. You can purchase the merchandise. But if you're buying the name, you must use a lawyer to make sure there aren't any liens on the name. You may want to put your own name that is similar to the one you're purchasing.

Incorporation

I get people that ask me, "Should I incorporate my business?"

It is simple; we just need to do the math. Incorporation is limiting your company to be its own legal company and getting it away from you personally. The lawyer will do up a minute book and a stamp for the company. Then you need to add to your company name, Ltd, Corp. Inc., or whatever you choose. This may cost about $1000 to $2000, and then every year you get a form from the government to fill out and a fee of about $ 60 to keep your incorporation.

If you are a business that is not incorporated then all the profits of your business will be added to your personal income taxes. With the formula of $40,000 profit and under, you will pay 24%, over $40,000 to $80,000 at 34%, and so on. But if you incorporate, the profits of the company pay 16%. However it stays in the company. As soon as you personally remove some money, you will pay personal taxes from 24 to 40% which ever your tax bracket is. So, if you add 24 plus 16, then you are paying 40%. But having it incorporated protects all your personal property from being taken in case of bankruptcy.

I know realtors go back and forth with this decision. I would incorporate a retail business.

It all depends on what you're doing with the money. If you have a lot of money coming in, at a high tax bracket, then incorporate at 16% and take out a small salary at 24%.

If you are self-employed, you will be paying CPP, FED tax and PRO tax, but you will also be paying the company portion of CPP, so remember this CPP company portion is tax deductible.

Chapter 7

Buying Real Estate Or Selling Or Renting/Leasing To Own

Purchasing

First you need money. If it is your first home, maybe some banks will give you no money down but there is a closing cost (lawyer fees, etc.). If it isn't your first home it would be 5% down. So don't forget putting 5% or more down is great but you also need money for lawyers, about ($1000.00 + adj. for the property taxes, water adj. and lots of fees for registration of the deed and other stuff. Your lawyer will do all these adjustments, and they will be on your invoice from the lawyer).

Your mortgage can have life insurance and property taxes added. At the bank, if you do not have 25% down on your mortgage, you will need to have your mortgage insured. This insurance rate will be added to your mortgage payments. These are some of the insurance companies that the banks often use like CHMC, Genworth Financial, etc. Did you know you can ask for a specific one!

Remember if you think your rent money will replace the mortgage payment, there is a lot more cost involved. When you are renting you cannot only look at the rent you pay compared to when you own your own home. You need to look at all other costs that come into play with a home, like water bills, home insurance, electric bills, etc. This can also make a big difference taking care of the property, lawn mower, snow blower. Fix and repair as you go. Things always need some attention, like painting and fixing your home to keep it up to date will cost money. You should always try to save some money each year in a fund to go toward the upkeep of your home. You will always need a roof in the future, and things can break down, such as your washer/dryer, fridge and stove. I don't think people realize the amount of money needed to run a home. Yes, the value also hopefully will go up, especially after 10 years. But make sure you purchase a home that is re-sellable so you don't lose any money (LOCATION, LOCATION). Also, I recommend using a realtor to purchase a property, especially for the first time buyers. They will help you make your decisions easier by helping you search and find exactly what you're looking for. They often have some inside information on most all the properties, such as if the seller is moving and needs to sell, or how long and why it has been sitting on the market, or if it had water in the basement, or it's in a bad neighborhood. They do all the negotiations, which can get ugly if there are any issues with the home. They help you get the best price and take care of all the paperwork.

The buyer will need to get information by certain dates; a finance letter should be first. You need to go to the bank and make sure they will lend you the money. Then inspection on the home, which can cost about $300 to $500; you can walk away if there are any problems. If the property has a well then a water test is needed; this will cost about $40 to $140. Remember the realtor is working for you for free; there is no charge for all their time looking for houses. The seller pays for all the realtor's fees. When looking for a home, make sure you study the location: Is it on a busy street? Can you hear the traffic if you're outside? I've noticed people looking for one particular type of home, which is fine but don't look at them all over town. First, decide how close do you want to be to your neighbors, how much land you want, where do you want to live from schools or how long of a commute do you want from your work? And if you have to cross bridges in busy morning traffic, remember buying a home is probably for long term and expensive (the average turn around in Canada is 7 years). But most people live there longer. The Baby Boomers are getting ready for retirement; the most popular home for this is a bungalow; one level living is going to be the best for resale. I'm not a big fan of really old homes; I like the wood details and the interior designs, but to live in them is less appealing to me. Because I find that you're spending money on new walls, new wiring and plumbing, and not on the décor. You almost have to rebuild the home at a certain point. Anything around 50 years or newer is good, but watch for the years were there was asbestos. What I commonly see more and more often is water in the basement. This can be for any reason, and most of it can be fixed, such as cracked foundation, a new sump pump, clogged drain tiles, etc. Drain tiles are pipes outside your home with holes that get the ground water and disperse it away from your foundation, and sometimes after 30 years or so they get full of dirt and tree roots. Watch for mildew. Often you see homes with mildew in the basement. It's very important to get a dehumidifier for the basement and keep it running to stop mildew. You should also have proper thickness of insulation in the attic about R40 rating is the new law to pass inspection.

If you're about to purchase a home that is in a flood zone, maybe you should pay attention to that. I bought a house and didn't think anything more about being in a flood zone because the last time it flooded was 1973. Guess what? I moved in August of 2007, and the next April my house was surrounded by water. The basement had 4 feet of water, my washer/dryer and couch were floating, and the house was surrounded by water. I lived in rubber boots for two weeks and spent over a month cleaning the mud off the stuff in the basement and from the basement floors.

Purchasing a condo is very common now with the retired people. There is no maintenance work required, and the value still goes up. Purchasing a new home is nice, but the home needs to settle and may get cracks in some of the tile work in the kitchen, if not done properly. The home also could get cracks in the walls and the foundation. The landscaping may not be done. Don't rush; buyer beware.

Selling

Selling can be a bit more difficult and very stressful. Once you have made the decision to sell, please realize that your home is now a "show case" for sale. People keep living normally, and their home will not show well. You need to remove all fridge magnets, keep stuff off the kitchen counter to make it look bigger, and remove all personal pictures or items. If you have holes in the wall it's best to remove your pictures and fix the hole and maybe give it a fresh neutral color of paint.

Remove all bright colors and paint with almond and beige colors; it will look richer. It's not too bad if your bathroom is a different color to match the tiles. Remember people just want to move in. If you want to give your home away at a great price then it is OK to leave it as is. Some people are looking for the deal to make it nice and maybe resell it later. You need to remember your home is "A SHOWROOM." You are just using the furniture and space for living, so pack and de clutter as much as possible. This will make your home sell faster; believe me, I know. Try to update your doorknobs and light fixtures; it's not very expensive, but it can make a big impact.

A large percentage of people can't see beyond a dated home. Selling can be very stressful if you're getting many calls to view. You need to remove the pets and the children and clean the home. Whether you're using a realtor or not, it can be time consuming. Always accommodate the purchaser's time to visit your home, even if it may not be perfectly clean; a showing is better than no showing. They will probably come back for a second viewing before they write an offer to see what they may want to negotiate into the deal. Once you get an offer, it will probably be low. Don't panic or get mad; everyone just wants the best deal. So counter the offer by a few thousand dollars and then wait to see how high the offer will get. It may not be the first, second, or even third counter offer but you will get closer to an agreed price. Sometimes if your home sits on the market too long, it is costing you money, so sacrificing a few thousand dollars on the deal may give you piece of mind just to have it sold. A vacant home can costs almost double in insurance. Using a realtor can help you; they pay for all the advertising, screen people and most realtors have people waiting for that perfect home. It just takes one person. You may say but the fees, however they are working for you to sell your home and helping you get the best price and have the most exposure and connection to sell your home. So you may have multiple offers if the price is right. You may get less, but it can be worth it, every month your house is not sold costs you money. The realtors will give you a free market analysis, which is a study of what sold in your neighborhood, and your street. They compare the same type of houses that sold and the ones that are still active. So here is a quick recap.

A. Most value for your home, paint and update

B. Keep clean

C. Use a realtor, for better exposure and marketing; they take the calls and do the paperwork

I notice that there aren't many homes for sale in the winter. People are always looking to buy; you would have less competition then. Remember the closing date doesn't have to be in the winter; you can close later. A lot of homes go on the market in April, so then by May and June everyone is reducing their homes. So if you're selling your home, put it on the market as soon as you have made this decision and keep it on the market until the house sells. It just takes one person to come along and buy your home. (Make sure you are priced right.)

Renting To Own

In case some people haven't heard of renting to own or leasing to own, here are some examples. If someone looking for a home and a home owner want to do a rent to own, you would sign some agreement papers with terms determined by the owner and the renter. All agreements will not be the same. If you cannot afford to buy a home and you can't make a down payment, the owner of the home you are interested in may want to do a rent to own agreement with you. Then you could live there with part of your monthly payment going towards your rent and the other part going towards the purchase price.

For example: your rent would be $800 per month and part of that rent would go toward the purchase price of the home. If your agreement was $500, this would go on the price of the home and the rest is interest or payment to the home owner (like rent). You also would pay all the expenses of the home as if you own it, property taxes; electric etc. the owner almost becomes a bank. So let's say you both agree on $150,000 for the home, and at the bank they are looking for $15,000 down payment (10%). But you don't have it so you rent the home for $500 per month on the principle on the home x 12 = $6000 per year x 3 years = $18,000 so now you may go see the bank and only need to get a mortgage on $132,000. That's what you owe to the homeowner. And only then your names are transferred to the home. If you don't make or miss a payment for the agreed amount of months, like 4 months, then the agreement is void and the owner keeps the home and money. The money you put down and any repairs or upgrades done to the property, you don't get back, just like a bank. Lawyers are not found of these deals because so many have gone bad. Some feel that the renter is taking a risk. But I think it is the property owner that is also taking a risk. He is left with whatever damage is done to the home.

Chapter 8

Personal Bankruptcy

Personal bankruptcy is not what people dream about. But if you're so deep into debt that you cannot pay your bill payments, not even by merging money, not even by lowering interest rates. If you can no longer keep up with all your debts, then maybe you need to declare personal bankruptcy. If you miss more than three payments on your home you also can lose your home to the bank; this is called bank repossession. I seem to start knowing more and more people that have filed for personal bankruptcy; it is a lot more common. Over 100,000 individuals in Canada file for personal bankruptcy per year.

There are companies with licensed trustees you must meet with that sit down with you and try to help you make these decisions and explain to you your obligations.

If you go online and search for Bankruptcy Canada, this is what they say.

(http://www.bankruptcy-canada.ca/bankruptcy/personal-bankruptcy.htm)

Your obligations are:

★ send monthly budget on how you
spent your money to the trustee.

★ make sure all your income taxes are filed each year.

★ attend two money classes

★ make monthly payment to your trustee

If you eliminate all other options and bankruptcy is the final option to solve your financial problems. Here are the **advantages and disadvantages of personal bankruptcy**

Bankruptcy provides these advantages:

Protects from collection action, legal

action and wage garnishees

Eliminates a person's unsecured debts

Is relatively quick

Can be inexpensive relative to the other options

On the other hand, bankruptcy has these disadvantages:

Is very hard on your credit history

(basically resets your credit history

to zero when completed)

May require you to surrender some pos-

sessions to your trustee

Requires you to keep detailed records of your

income and expenses while you remain bankrupt.

Although bankruptcy adversely affects a person's credit rating, most people going into bankruptcy have such a bad credit rating that nothing will make it worse. In fact, after bankruptcy, a person is a better credit risk because he or she has no debt. Personal bankruptcy is a powerful vehicle for a debtor to get a fresh financial start.

When might personal bankruptcy be necessary for you?If you are a resident of Canada who is unable to pay your bills when they are due, and you have tried everything possible to get back on your feet, it may be time to consider personal bankruptcy.

Anyone who owes more than $1,000 is eligible for personal bankruptcy in Canada. Ideal candidates are those who need a rapid financial fresh start.

Filing for bankruptcy is a difficult decision. It will eliminate most, if not all of your debts, but it will also hinder your ability to obtain credit in the future.

How much you own:

You will lose all your money and possessions, except for the assets that are exempt in your province.

How much you earn and your family size:

You will lose part of any earnings which are considered "surplus income" – that is, anything over a limit set by law. The limit depends on your earnings level and your family size, according to a complex formula. When you see your trustee, bring your latest pay stubs, to allow the trustee to estimate how much you must pay based on surplus income.

Costs of the bankruptcy process:

Bankruptcy involves administrative costs, including court fees, mailing costs, and government-set fees for filing. You will probably be required by your trustee to pay these costs.

Other costs:

Taxes work differently in a bankruptcy, and your trustee will give you any details that apply to you. For example, any GST credits or tax refunds that would normally come to you while bankrupt will be lost to your bankrupt estate.

You will also lose any "windfalls" you receive or become entitled to while bankrupt. "Windfalls" are amounts you get by luck, such as inheritance or lottery winnings.

Cost of bankruptcy in your case:

More than you can pay? You will need a bankruptcy trustee to determine exactly how *much it will cost you to go bankrupt in Canada* and what alternatives to bankruptcy would make sense in your case.

What to do after bankruptcy?

After my bankruptcy requirements are completed, what happens?

When you complete all your duties in bankruptcy, you will obtain a type of discharge, which is the official certification of how it was completed.

Your personal bankruptcy will be a permanent part of your life history. When asked if you have been bankrupt, you must always answer "yes". To do otherwise would be fraud.

A record of your bankruptcy will remain on your credit report (from the credit bureaus) for several years after your discharge.

Apart from the note of your past bankruptcy, your credit status will be clear. It will be as if you had never had credit.

Like a young adult starting independent life, you will have to earn the trust of creditors from the ground up.

Financial life after bankruptcy – Can I get credit again?

After bankruptcy, it will probably take three to five years for you to get access to new credit again. Your best strategy during this period is to manage your financial affairs wisely. Build the strongest position you can, by earning a steady income and living within your means.

If you were able to keep your house and your mortgage payments are up-to-date, you can probably renew your mortgage without difficulty at any time after bankruptcy. Continuing the mortgage and keeping the payments current will make a valuable contribution to building a good credit rating again.

Similarly, if you want a new secured loan for a car or house, the lender will be mostly interested in your having a steady income to support the payments, and the security you can offer.

Even while the bankruptcy still shows on your credit report, you can start to get unsecured credit again, if you follow a careful process to gradually and deliberately repair your credit.

Of course, you should make sure that you understand your credit report, and take any needed steps to get it updated and corrected.

Feelings and thoughts after your bankruptcy

After you complete your bankruptcy, the burden of debts you can't pay will be wiped out. Most people experience a great feeling of relief at finally achieving that fresh financial start they needed so much.

The lessons you have learned will be valuable for your future success. You must know that the ways you handled money need to be changed, and the credit counselling you received during bankruptcy will have given you new abilities to do better with money. Whether you actually do so is now up to you. Will you follow the help and good advice you have received?

Not been bankrupt yet?

If you have not yet filed for bankruptcy as a solution to your difficulties, reading this page was wise. I advise everyone with money problems to research personal bankruptcy and bankruptcy alternatives, so as to make the best possible decision.

Asked questions:

Does filing for bankruptcy in Canada affect My spouse?

Filing for bankruptcy in Canada does not directly affect your spouse. Your debts are your debts; only you are responsible for them. If you go bankrupt, your debts are discharged. Your husband or wife or common-law spouse is NOT responsible for your debts.

Many people believe that because you are married, your spouse is automatically responsible for your debts. This is not true. Often collection agents, when they are trying to collect from you, tell you that if you don't pay they will get the money from your spouse. This is a collection agency scare tactic; they can only go after you for your debts.

The only exception is if your spouse has co-signed or guaranteed your debt. For example, if you took out a loan and your spouse co-signed for it, it is also legally their loan. If you both have a credit card on the same account, the credit card debt legally belongs to both of you.

Remember, your spouse is liable for the debt, not because they are your spouse, but because they have signed for the debt. (I bold this because I think it is very important.)

If all of your debts are in your name, your bankruptcy will not affect your spouse's credit rating. However, the bankrupt spouse may not qualify as a co-signer in the future due to the bankruptcy, so one spouse's bankruptcy may have an indirect impact on the other spouse.

What happens to my debts when I go bankrupt in Canada?

What happens to your debts when you go bankrupt in Canada is complex. It depends on the type of debt, and in some cases on your payment status. There are actually some debts that stay, even in bankruptcy.

The concept behind a personal bankruptcy in Canada is relatively simple. When you file for bankruptcy, you surrender your assets in return for the discharge of your debts. Just as there are some bankruptcy exemptions from losing all your assets, there are some exceptions to the discharge of all your debts. Both are affected when debts are secured by assets, as in a mortgage.

Unsecured debts

In general, bankruptcy will discharge all your unsecured debts, but the law makes exceptions for **these debts that stay**:

Student loans less than 10 years old

Child and spousal support

Fines and most court ordered restitution payments

Court awarded damages for sexual assault or intentionally inflicting bodily harm

Debts that arose as a result of fraud or theft

Certain government overpayments

In a bankruptcy, here are some examples of **debts that go away**:

Credit card balances

Lines of credit (if unsecured)

Personal loans (if unsecured)

Arrears of income taxes and municipal house taxes

Unpaid utility bills

Retail store accounts

Insurance premiums past due

Medical bills

Payday loans

How long will I be bankrupt in Canada?

Several factors affect the *length of your bankruptcy in Canada.* Your bankruptcy ends when you receive a discharge, the event that actually cancels your debts.

Most bankrupts in Canada are eligible for discharge after the minimum period of nine months. Your bankruptcy will last for more than nine months if the bankruptcy court orders your bankruptcy extended.

Here are the conditions that could prolong your bankruptcy:

Do you have surplus income?

If your income is considerably higher than the limits set by the government, it is possible that your bankruptcy will be extended for longer than nine months.

Is this your first bankruptcy?

If you have been bankrupt before, you are not eligible for an automatic discharge from bankruptcy in nine months. Your bankruptcy will be extended for a period of time that will be determined by a judge or registrar of the bankruptcy court.

Have you completed all your duties as a bankrupt person?

If you have failed to complete one or more of your duties in bankruptcy, then your discharge will be delayed. The delay will depend on the seriousness of the failure and how soon you complete the missing duties.

Is your discharge opposed?

The discharge is usually granted if you are earning only enough income to keep yourself and your dependants reasonably provided for, and if you have received credit counselling.

Occasionally, creditors, the trustee, or the superintendent of bankruptcy oppose a bankrupt's discharge. When this happens, the matter goes to mediation or is heard before a registrar or a judge.

Get your trustee's advice

Your bankruptcy trustee will discuss the likely length of your bankruptcy with you during your first meeting, and will help you to keep it as short as possible.

Bankruptcy Alternatives

You can't pay your bills, and solutions you have considered include. Here are some more alternatives.

When you can't pay your bills

Non-payment is a non-option! You may feel so overwhelmed enough that you just try to carry on without paying. This will only make matters worse:

One payment missed: IF you have a good borrowing history, your creditors may simply send you a polite reminder letter.

Two payments missed: You will get a strongly worded letter, and possibly also phone calls, demanding payment.

Three payments missed: Each creditor will enlist a collection agency to press you for payment. Collection agencies will make your life unpleasant, using a variety of tactics to get the money, including threats.

If you still don't pay, stronger methods can be used against you.

Your best bet to make things better is to **act immediately**.

Chapter 9

Bookeeping

Anyone who is self-employed needs to keep records of all transaction for their business. Many people may be putting all or most of their receipts in a shoe box, the ones that they can find and then dropping it off at their accountant, but this is very expensive. Accountants charge a lot per hour to sort these receipts.

To anyone who is a realtor, a contractor, a baby sitter, or a hairdresser, etc., if you own your own business, big or small, you should learn how to do your own bookkeeping. There aren't a lot of fans of the accounting world, but for those of you who want to know how it works, here is a little lesson.

You would need a column book, or if you're good at Excel on the computer, you can create your own. You can also use computer programs like Simply Accounting that help you.

You always need to balance the columns to zero. They have their own purposes. Some are debts (DR), and the others are credits (CR). In other words, use minuses and pluses to balance to zero.

Writing something in a book or on a computer is called "posting"; you start by posting your entry in the column that the money would have come from. Did you write a cheque? Then you would post out of (BANK) CR. Or did you pay cash then post out of (CASH) CR column? Then you look at what it is. Is it a telephone bill? And did you pay HST on the bill? These numbers would have to go into their own columns that said (HST) DR and (TELEPHONE) DR. For example:

Date	Description	BANK CR	HST DR	Telephone DR
April 13	Telephone ck# 34	123.45	14.20	109.25
So Cr 123.45 – 14.20DR–109.25 DR must equal to 0.				

Credit on the bank means it came out of the bank from a cheque, and DR means it came into the bank as a deposit. HST has also DR and CR. When you receive payments/ money (sales from your business), they paid you HST, so that would be posted in (CR). And when you paid someone HST (from your expenses telephone, gas, etc...) it would be (DR), This is an expense to you. So you will see most of all the columns like phone, rent, salary to employees, office supplies, misc., car, purchaser (suppliers of products you purchase), etc., would all be DR.

So the example I just gave you has to balance with the full amount of the telephone bill that you paid. The amount out of the bank then is broken down to HST that you paid, and the actual amount of the telephone charges are posted in telephone as DR. Then add all the DR and minus all from the CR and this has to equal zero.

So this would be what your column book would look like:

Cash Dr,|| Cash Cr,|| Visa Cr,|| (or Master Card) ,||Bank Dr,|| Bank Cr,||HST CR||HST DR|| Sale Cr,|| Telep Dr,|| office DR,|| Purchaser Dr,|| shipping Dr,||Auto Dr,|| Gas DR,|| Adv, Dr,|| Fees or int DR,|| Misc. Dr||.....etc to whatever relates to your business.

Note: Gas for your car and auto repairs cannot be claimed 100% unless you leave the vehicle at all times at your business. If at any moment you use your vehicle for personal use, then you determine the breakdown. Realtors should be around 90%. Also, for people that bring clients out to eat in their own town or if you are out of town on business, you can only claim 50% on food.

If you have a designated place for an office, such as realtors who work for their company and have an office, you cannot claim any home office even if you work out of your home, most of the time, because you have a home base for the company. Your head office would have to be in a different town for you to be able to claim any home office.

Designate a page or a tab if you're on Excel, for every month even if it isn't full.

I would take a back page to calculate the food and auto/gas breakdown and then transfer it to the right month as a posting.

Keep all your receipt in different folders with all the same types of receipts together, such as credit cards, bank statements, etc.

When paying your HST, you must calculate your entire sale for three months. Add this number to the form, and then add all your HST CR for the three months required, and then add all your HST debts. Then do your CR minus to your DR, and if you get a plus you need to pay the government that amount; if you get a credit (-) you will send the form in and get paid this amount in a cheque.

The thing is by keeping your own records, you will be on top of your business and will be able to see if you're spending more than you are earning. Also, I made a chart with the sales of my business every month. If you do this, then you know the lowest months in sales for your business, so that you can advertise in these months to bring up sales.

Chapter 10

Let's Talk

It is so funny sometimes when you think about what schools are teaching us, history, cutting up a frog, math, gym, languages, etc. There are lots of things you need to learn for your future. But then everyone goes out into this world without having any knowledge of finance. We spend the rest of our lives working with money every day; it controls all our decisions, it gives us a future and, it gives us a roof over our head and food to survive. The most important thing we all have to do in this world is WORK WITH MONEY, and no one teaches us the consequences and the rewards of money. Then we have to live and learn and make the best of it. Once you're in your 40's and have made some mistakes, wouldn't it have been great to start over and make better decisions from what you've learned? If only we would have known where to put it, and how to spend it right, at a younger age. Now at 40 you could have been a millionaire, happy and healthy, which would help our health care system. Imagine having a class in school that would discuss money and getting rich, RRSPs, TFSA, GICs, and how to write a cheque. Hopefully this book will be a great tool to get some of those answers and provide knowledge of money and will help readers be able to make better decisions when going forward. It was my dream to write this book; getting it into print was a big step for me. I took the chance and spent the money, and I just needed to do it. Helping people with money issues is my lifelong dream, and it consumes me.

I was looking at some courses in the paper, and I noticed one about "Effective Public Speaking". My body was halfway into a panic attack because I'm very shy and public speaking is one of my biggest fears. The other half said you have to take this course. I struggled with this decision all weekend, and then I thought it is only 8 hours of my life and it can only change it for the better. So I called. That was it; it was done, and I had to go.

Wednesday night I arrived at the class. The teacher greeted me with a handshake and a hello. There were a few more women there, and we ended up with ten women of all ages, from 20's to 60's. The first day we had to introduce ourselves in front of the class behind a podium. We had to talk for one and a half minutes. I was the fourth person to go up and speak. I was not sure what to say, so I just started talking about my life, where I lived, and how I got to the city of Fredericton.

When you speak you are not really aware of the people looking at you; you are more aware of what you're going to say. After I finished I almost felt like I wanted to go back and talk some more, but only for a few seconds; the fear was still there the next week. The teacher was great because he talked calmly to us and made it very easy. (Thanks, Steven.) The next two weeks we had random questions to pick from, and we had 1 minute and 30 seconds to talk about our answer.

It got easier to talk in front of people. But then in the last class, we had to do a prepared speech for two and a half minutes. So, of course, I had to talk about MONEY, my strongest subject. Here is my speech.

"Good evening, ladies and gentlemen. My name is Denise LeBlanc.

There is one thing that frustrates me more and more each day. In school we learn about history, languages, math, biology, and chemistry. We even had to take gym. The fact that I had to take a science course and dissect a frog made me question its use. What did that give me in life? What is the one thing that everyone uses, everyone needs, and our whole life depends on it? MONEY, money. Why wouldn't we have to take a class where we dissect money? Like classes on how to save for the future, on RRSP, on budgeting, and how to respect money. Money is present in everything we do in life. It means food, and it means our survival, and no one teaches us anything about managing money. How many people do you know that have their future planned out? People who have savings for their next car, or for home repairs, or for retirement? Do you think if people would have learned how to manage money at an early age that we wouldn't be seeing so many problems with people losing their homes, getting in bad debts, and having no money at retirement? It frustrates me to see about 70% of people not having any knowledge about any bank products available to them. I was talking to someone the other day; he was 48 years old and was thinking he should start looking at RRSPs. He didn't know anything about TFSA, GIC, or even mutual funds. People should know this at an early age. They could have been putting money away for their retirement in their 20's, and they would be in great financial shape. They could have 1 million dollars at retirement. With the magic of compound interest and time, your money can also work for you. So learn as much as possible about managing money because your future and your children's future depend on it."

I was the last speaker before the break, and I got a little nervous during my speech. I think my hands were shaking a bit. I don't remember my performance. But once I sat down at my seat two women, one in her 50's and the other in her 60's, came over to talk to me with big smiles on their faces saying, "Yes, that is so true." One woman said her daughter went bankrupt 3 times, and she wished she would have known me years ago. They both asked, "Where were you years ago?" She said nobody talked about money in the past; it was private. Parents never shared this with their children. They only learned about money products later in life. Then I realized that the teacher was talking about money with one of the girls in the front row, and I heard my name. And two more girls turned to say something about money also. So this just seals the deal for writing this book. I could talk about money all day every day.

I was talking to someone today about a small town guy who made it big in the baseball National League. He was also very good as a hockey player but chose to go pro in base-ball. The town he grew up in was very small, outside of a one store town. He went on to make it big. The person I was talking to was also a very good athlete, but didn't go on to play professionally, mostly because he was very poor and he quit school in grade 10. He started working and hanging out with friends. The parents or the schools didn't push him to "go for his dream". He was told to go to work. Today, I find that parents are more likely to get their kids into higher educa-tions and to join more sports. Back in the 1960's and 1970's, they didn't push these things as much. Today you should do the best you can. If it is your dream, remember only you can push to make it happen. Because this guy could have been great, and I'm sure we lose a lot of potential people in everything, from sports, to singing, and other great talents because of them being so young and not knowing any better. Parents and teachers should encourage them.

At work we have a morning minute every day to help us be better and inspire us. For example, here are some great words from a great speaker, Richard Flint. He is one of America's top personal development speakers and coaches.

I read Richard Flint every morning and it has greatly help me in my life. Thank you RICHARD.

"You were put on this earth to be creative, to seek adventure, and to see how much presence you can have. Hey, if you go to your grave never fully achieving what you were put on this earth to achieve, did you actually live?"

"Ninety eight percent of all depression is personal, not clinical. Personal depression is the result of not being able to see, to feel and experience the good in life. When the good is celebrated, there is the bubbling of inspiration, which creates the flow of energy that results in momentum; with that you can't be depressed. Why? Because there's too much to celebrate."

"Question—do you have a dream for your life? Now, I'm not talking about statements you keep making about "someday," but an actual plan for your life you're working on? Your mind is about adventure. It is about turning your imagination loose to soar with ideas and adventures that fill you with enthusiasm in being alive. Without that, you will get up each day trying to figure out your meaning of life.

Remember, opportunities are always present, but you must be ready for them"

"Waiting is just another form of procrastination. So many state what they want to achieve and then, just sit down and wait. If you want success for your life, you must seek it. You must be willing to get up, take the positive actions and move forward with disciplined determination. Waiting won't achieve that."

"Find your dream, don't get to the end of your earthly time and wonder what you could have done or been, or what you could have achieved. Achieve it now."

He inspires us all with his great words.

The 3 rules I live buy

1. Don't go into a partnership in business.
2. Don't co-sign on loans for anyone.
3. Don't lend any money to anyone, especially close friends or family. (Give it to them without expecting anything back; if they have any morals they will give it back.)

Of course, I broke rule one and two, and this just reestablished the reason I have these rules.

Thank you for reading this book. This means you are hopefully better knowledge on how to make your dreams come true. *I hope you have great success and live your life to the fullest....*

Introduction of

Financial Freda (Cartoon Character)

As Financial Freda is given the OK, she walks onto a high school stage.

"Hello everybody, how are you all today? Are you all glad to be missing a class? I know you have to listen to someone talking about money, but give me one hour of your time. I'm hoping to change the rest of your life." As a successful financial expert, Freda is always asked to speak in schools, teaching high school kids the basics of how life and money is very important, and how it changes everything.

(My middle name is Freda, and it is my mother's name. I wanted to create a cartoon character that brings my passions out. I hope you enjoy Financial Freda and some other characters that I have created.)

"I would like to talk to you about LIFE first. What I find when talking to people is that people just seem to be living day to day, not thinking of their future. WHERE are you? And WHERE are you going? If you were dealt a bad hand in life and you think, that's just the way it is, and you think you cannot change anything about it, well you are wrong. You have the power to change everything about your life, health, money, and happiness. If you choose to be negative about life or think that you're too stupid, or blame others for your failures, you will never get a positive outcome in life. If you have a positive outlook and take control of your life and do all the things you want, then you (with hard work) can have all your dreams come true. Your positive new outlook in life will change everything. Feeling great and thinking better will bring great health and wealth for you so you can be the happiest person possible in this world.

We all make mistakes with life and money, so we just need to keep adjusting and always try to make it better."

"It's hard work and no one really teaches us about life and money, and our minds just don't want to deal with these things. It should be something taught at a young age just like walking and talking, teaching strength and independence. It's not only a grown up responsibility. Everyone's responsible for themselves. I see so many people not even worried about money or their future; it's as if it was someone else's job to do this. IT IS only your job to TAKE CARE OF YOURSELF. If more women and men would be strong enough in their self-confidence and take care of their future, they may not be so caught up in bad relationships or in relationships for money. IT IS NOT THE MAN'S JOB TO TAKE CARE OF THE WOMAN or vice-versa. Please get strong, get educated, get healthy, and be happy. Save your money and make yourself proud that you will never need anyone to take care of you, just someone to love you. In today's society we have all the tools to make these things happen."

"So again let's recap just in case you fell asleep." The kids laugh and get back up straight in their seats as they had slid down.

"Repeat after me...We live life to the best and strongest way possible. We need to take care of ourselves for the future."

"Now that you're all awake, I want to give you a book for you to take home and fill out the information in the best way possible. Remember it needs to come from you. No one else is responsible for your future but you. Then return it to your homeroom teacher in two days, and she will make sure that you filled it out. Then she will return them to you for you to keep and hopefully follow your own words and dreams you've set out for yourself for your future."

"Now we need to respect and learn about money. It's very important that the word respect is always used when talking about money. Look around you, your clothes your shoes, this building that you are sitting in. It all needs to be here for us to give you a future, and this can only happen with money. Otherwise, you would be sitting naked on the land that mother earth left us to live in. You are so lucky to be in this country, but you need to work to live and eat. The opportunities are here for you to take advantage of."

"As you see I'm wearing balls around my waist, these back chains and black balls represent good debt (in the black), like properties (home mortgages debts), because they increase in value and you can sell them. The red balls represent consumer debt, credit cards, car loans, just bad debt. See my pair of golden slippers over there," as she points out on the stage. "That's where we are all going someday, the golden years of retirement, and hopefully we will not be carrying these red balls with us. TIME is everything. You don't need to have everything today. If you take your time and pay cash for your little things as you go you will be so much happier with your life, and health (and no money stress) is the key to happiness."

"So all together, NO MORE RED BALLS, NO MORE RED BALLS. We need to make sure you understand the importance of not having any red balls. You will be wasting precious money on interest that could hold you back from getting your dreams, hopefully bigger and better things in life."

Financial Freda Work Booklet

What are your favorite things in life that you want in the future? Put them in order starting with the most important:

1) _____, 2)_____, 3)_____,
4) _____, 5) _____.

Example:	
Own your own business.	Early retirement
Health (stay in shape)	Travel
Family (children)	Favorite car, bike or boat etc…
HomeMoney	(1 million at retirement)
Cottage	Security (get a great job)

…. Or more, whatever your dreams are, write them down.

How will you make them happen? What do you think you need to do to get these dreams to become reality? What time line do you give yourself?

1) _____ time line (goal)_____

2) _____ time line (goal)_____

3) _____ time line (goal)_____

4) _____ time line (goal)_____

5) _____ time line (goal)_____

   (My Example) 1) *Early Retirement at age 50, plus work part time till 58.*

You need to give yourself a reasonable time line or you won't do it. And keep checking your goal; you should look at this every year, either on your birthday or Jan. 1. And check off the ones you have accomplished.

Also I would like for you to see this example for owning a house with expected expenses you need to be aware of.

$ 200,000 Home

Payments: mortgage (minus -5% down) with 5% interest = about $950 per month payment

Power: avg. $350 per month

Tax: avg. $2500 per year ($208 per month)

Insurance: avg. $1000.00 per year ($83 per month)

Water: avg. $800 per year ($67 per month)

Upkeep: avg. $1000 per year ($83 per month)

Like gas lawn mower, snow blower or if you hired someone lawn care flower trees, misc. etc.

So let just do a little math here; $ 1741 per month, ARE you in shock? You can adjust your house payment, but make sure you get all these prices before you purchase a home.

Now the rest of your money goes on car payment, car insurance, gas, groceries, some in savings (if possible), and, if applicable, don't forget the children's and the pet's needs.

   Do you feel rich?

   After one hour, Freda is wrapping it up!

"That's all for me today. Take care and I hope you all have a happy, healthy, wealthy, and stress free life." Everyone gets up and applauds as she nods her head and walks off stage.

Financial Freda gives seminars on finance at the high schools meeting some awesome characters like Budget Betty, Partying Paul, Tight Tommy and Shopping Sharon. She also does a half hour TV show with some great guests, and, of course, she asks the most personal questions, such as "What are you doing with your MONEY?" People should be proud to talk about money because it inspires more people to talk about it and better understand what is out there and what some people are doing with their life.

Introduction: Who are you most similar to?

Budget Betty: watches her money to get better things in life, and is getting to financial freedom and security. (Good going.)

Partying Paul: enjoys life every day and lives day to day, drinks, smokes, and parties all weekend but still wants nice toys. (Hope you get a good job!)

Tight Tommy: saves everything and hates to spend money, others will usually pay for him, will never pay for other people. (Good luck keeping friends.)

Shopping Sharon: loves to spend money on herself, looks good, has no concept of money and debt and never thinks of the future, always thinks there will always be money in the future. (Wait till you're 50; you'll get a wakeup call. Can you say consumer debt?).

Betty will go to parties with Paul, but she doesn't drink or smoke but is still having fun being with people having fun. Tommy goes out to taverns with his friends but everyone just pays for their own drinks. Sharon is always having fun with her friends, and she thinks she doesn't spend money.

It doesn't matter who you are or where you come from. It just matters who you want to be in your forties and fifties. So you need to start young to get your life together, and your dreams will come true. Everyone can do it, never say no, be positive, and start making changes for the better.

Here is Financial Freda, looking her best with long brown hair and wearing her "No More Red Balls" t-shirt and a pair of jeans. She gets to the stage of her show and sits on a high stool and has a little desk that rolls in front of her when needed. The desk looks like a stool with long legs with wheels, and the top looks like a little wooden desk. It almost reminds me of the hairdressers rolling trays they use for holding stuff. Let's listen to her starting her show.

"Hello everyone, welcome to my show, 'Let's Talk Money' Hope you're all ready to meet a famous hockey player that is coming on the show today. We will surely have fun with him. For now, let's first talk about money that is making the news. Well, some banks have lowered their rate to 2.99%; . Hey everyone who has a home line, run and lock some money in now, or if you're looking to buy a home; go lock that rate in. The only bad thing is the future, will you be ready to pay your mortgage if it jumps up 2 or 3% more? This low interest rate is really bad for people who are retiring, or have money in the bank and want to get the dividends out to live on.

"Oh well let's see what the rich and famous are up to...so let's welcome Chris Kobe to the stage. He is out of play from his hockey team with a concussion, and we are very happy he had time to visit today." Clapping, clapping, he gives a hug to Freda and has a seat. "Hello Mr. Kobe, thank you very much for taking the time to come here and visit with us. Do you know what kind of show this is…. Or is your concussion throwing you off?"

"Yes Freda, I know, you help people with money and not only money but making their dreams come true. When I was young, I always played hockey and wanted to play with the NHL, of course. It is the dream of a lot of young children, and I wanted to come here and tell everyone that you CAN have your dreams come true. Yes, it may take a long time and a lot of hard work, but it is always possible if you don't give up."

"I hear you live and breathe hockey. Do you think that is the major key to your success?" asks Freda

"Well it doesn't hurt to give it your all and work hard to become the best that you can be at whatever you are doing. Some people have more natural talent and some have to work harder; it's like music, some have the gift and some need to practice more," says Chris.

"By the way, are you putting at least 10% away for your future? You know you're still very young, and it doesn't matter how much money you make; it's what you do with it that counts," says Freda.

"Well, yes I have been putting some away because, you know, hockey doesn't last until 65," says Chris

After 30 minutes of talking with Chris, Freda stands up and says:

"I would like to thank you again for coming, and I am a great fan of yours. Wish you a speedy recovery and hope to see you play again soon!"

Chris gets up and waves to the audience, walking away. Everyone is clapping.

Freda walks over to the open stage and puts her belt with plastic chains that has a ball attached to the end of it. This belt carries some red and black painted Styrofoam balls on her waist. Some are red and some are black. She addresses the audience: "I think we should take some red paper or color it red to represent red balls. Then put them somewhere where you would see them every day. Put them on the mirror or on the wall of your bedroom. When you wake up and go to sleep you will see them. So take your cut up paper and mark on your ball a 1, 5 or 10 for every $1000, $5,000 or $10,000 in consumer debt. Your goal is to remove all the balls and not to add some on! With your new budget, that will get you started on paying your debt, you will be able to start remove your paper balls so you can see yourself in the mirror, ha-ha. See each black ball is a debt that weighs you down but is a good debt, like your home mortgage or any real estate. Your red balls are the bad debt that you need to worry about in life and not bring over to retirement."

Freda has t-shirts made that have a red ball and chain with a red line across it. Freda says,

"That is all for me, hope you all had a good time today, and you feel a little closer to taking steps to make your dreams come true. Good night and be safe."

Freda is coming off stage. Her producer says, "Hi we had a great show, the guest was great…" Freda sits down with the producer, and they start talking about future shows.

Freda mentions, "Let's get some bankers, teachers, parents, people that have gone bankrupt, millionaires, retired people to see how they are doing in this economy. Maybe see if children are even thinking about money."

The producer replies, "Great ideas, we will work on this. I'll see you later."

Freda nods and walks away.

She has great passion for helping people and wanting to see everyone succeed in getting the best out of life.

www.ingramcontent.com/pod-product-compliance
Lightning Source LLC
Chambersburg PA
CBHW051446280526
45785CB00003B/1452